Interactive Handbook for Understanding Reading Diagnosis

Interactive Handbook for Understanding Reading Diagnosis

A Problem-Solving Approach Using Case Studies

Kathy Roskos
John Carroll University

Barbara J. Walker
Eastern Montana College

Merrill, an imprint of
Macmillan Publishing Company
New York

Maxwell Macmillan Canada
Toronto

Maxwell Macmillan International
New York   Oxford   Singapore   Sydney

Cover art: © Marjory Dressler/Photographics
Editor: Linda James Scharp
Production Editor: Linda Hillis Bayma
Art Coordinator: Lorraine Woost
Photo Editor: Anne Vega
Cover Designer: Cathleen Norz
Production Buyer: Pamela D. Bennett

This book was set in Serifa by Compset, Inc. and was printed and bound by Semline, Inc., a Quebecor America Book Group Company. The cover was printed by Phoenix Color Corp.

Macmillan Publishing Company
866 Third Avenue
New York, NY 10022

Macmillan Publishing Company is part of the
Maxwell Communication Group of Companies.

Maxwell Macmillan Canada, Inc.
1200 Eglinton Avenue East, Suite 200
Don Mills, Ontario M3C 3N1

Library of Congress Cataloging-in-Publication Data
Roskos, Kathy.
    Interactive handbook for understanding reading diagnosis : a problem-solving approach using case studies / Kathy Roskos, Barbara J. Walker.
        p.   cm.
    Includes bibliographical references and index.
    ISBN 0-02-423730-2
    1. Reading (Elementary)—United States—Case studies.   2. Reading (Elementary)—United States—Problems, exercises, etc.   3. Reading (Elementary)—United States—Ability testing—Case studies.
    I. Title.
    LB1573.R66   1994
    372.4'14—dc20   93-10120
                                                                      CIP

Printing: 1 2 3 4 5 6 7 8 9   Year: 4 5 6 7 8

Photo credits: Philip D. Roskos, p. 18; Barbara Schwartz, p. 26.

Preface

Interactive Handbook for Understanding Reading Diagnosis: A Problem-Solving Approach Using Case Studies is a book for preservice and inservice teachers enrolled in reading courses, particularly those courses dealing with reading diagnosis. This book presents a hands-on approach to developing the concepts and skills associated with assessing and instructing children and youth who encounter difficulties with reading. Through a series of interactive activities and case studies, those using this book become engaged in a variety of problem-solving tasks that stress two points: (1) reading is a process whereby individuals construct meaning with print, and (2) diagnosis is a process whereby teachers observe, analyze, interpret, and translate information about readers' behaviors into instructional action, then reflect about their own decision making.

The purpose of this book is to assist preservice and inservice teachers in their understanding of reading diagnosis and its ongoing use in literacy instruction. In a somewhat novel way, students are introduced to the concepts underlying reading diagnosis and are given opportunities to apply them to case studies of real-life reading situations and problems.

This text is considered a supplement to a course in reading diagnosis. It is assumed that preservice teachers have had at least one course in reading/language arts methods prior to beginning this text, and that a core text is also required reading. The activities will extend the student's knowledge of reading and diagnostic processes. Throughout the text, other textbooks are referenced. Many of them would provide an excellent core text. Additionally, the accompanying instructor's guide has additional activities and examples of responses to help in explaining the key concepts. It is hoped that this text will provide you and your students with a more active college classroom, where ideas can be tried out, exchanged, and modified so that learning becomes more meaningful and personalized.

All of the interactive activities presented grew out of our own experiences as teachers of reading diagnosis. They represent a discovery approach to learning content related to diagnostic activity. In meeting new ideas in this way, students are invited to learn by doing rather than through reading and discussion alone. We do utilize discussion; we believe students need to discuss, in cooperative learning groups, what they did and how they completed the activities. As they discuss, they reconstruct their understanding, articulating what they know and integrating it into the decision-making process. By "talking through" and explaining their thinking, new ideas and strategies become part of their internal thought processes.

PART ONE

This book is divided into four parts. In Part One, the fundamentals of diagnosis are discussed. These include an understanding of how reading develops from birth, an understanding of the intricacies of the reading process, a familiarity with the thinking skills central to the diagnostic process, and an awareness of a variety of diagnostic tools and procedures. Specifically, the following main ideas are developed:

◆ Reading is a problem-solving process that includes predicting, confirming, and integrating behaviors.
◆ There are milestones in children's literacy development.
◆ One's own beliefs about reading influence one's literacy teaching.
◆ Diagnosis is a problem-solving process that includes theorizing behaviors (observation, analysis, interpretation, translation, and reflection).
◆ Teachers use a variety of assessment tools and analytic procedures in reading diagnosis.

Also in Part One, readers are introduced to case studies involving individual readers and teachers. We view these as "first-level" case studies, since their intent is to acquaint the student with basic knowledge about diagnosis by using cases as examples of the content of diagnosis. The case studies simply present the content in a general and straightforward way.

PART TWO

Part Two of the book focuses on instruction, describing an array of teaching techniques that develop readers' print and meaning processing strategies. An instructional routine is also presented, providing an example of how diagnosis can become ongoing in daily literacy instruction. In the course of examining the instructional routine, coherence and balance in lesson design are emphasized. The chapters in Part Two address the following points:

◆ Readers process print and meaning.
◆ Teachers use specific techniques to develop readers' abilities to process print and meaning successfully.
◆ An instructional routine can facilitate the integration of diagnosis into literacy teaching.

The case studies in Part Two support and extend the students' knowledge of instruction, culminating in an in-depth critique of a reading lesson. They are designed to create mental images of teaching so that students can more readily relate to the procedures of instruction.

PART THREE

Part Three involves the reader in applying the diagnostic process to individual problem readers and small groups. Following a review of this process, a different kind of case study is used to develop problem-solving and decision-making skills related to diagnosis. Students analyze and interpret cases that develop ideas in four areas.

◆ Teachers judiciously select assessment tools to conduct observations of readers' behaviors.
◆ They analyze data, generating summary statements to faciliate their analysis.
◆ Teachers interpret their findings, looking for patterns in readers' behaviors.
◆ They translate their interpretations into practice as they choose appropriate instructional techniques and reflect about their choices.

PART FOUR

Part Four addresses other practical issues surrounding reading assessment and instruction, namely standardized testing and the management of diagnostic information. In Chapter Nine, case studies are used in yet a different manner. These case studies ask students to reflect critically on ambiguous situations that require making ethical decisions based on theoretical constructs. Chapter Ten focuses on organizing and maintaining diagnostic data, presenting three systems of information management. Together, these chapters develop the following concepts:

◆ The joint use of formal and informal assessments enlarges our understanding of readers' behaviors.
◆ The use of multiple sources of information (formal and informal) improves communication with colleagues, parents, and children.
◆ Careful and organized handling of diagnostic information conveys an attitude of respect for readers' performance from multiple data sources.

How This Book Was Developed

For several years, we have been experimenting with ways to change our instructional approach in the college classroom. We, like others in our field, had found that the lecture format created passive, rather than active, learners. For a couple of our lectures, we began by sharing activities that we had used. This sharing led to designing and using case studies in various formats to teach the major concepts in the course. The result has been a set of interactive activities that can be used, along with a more traditional approach, to teach preservice students concepts about the reading diagnosis process. In the last three years, through our use of these activities in conjunction with a core text, we have found that our students have become more active thinkers and are more willing to take risks and to use their newly developed knowledge to solve complex instructional problems.

How to Use This Book

This book approaches learning in a unique fashion. Interactive activities are designed so that they build on one another. With each successive activity, ideas and skills presented earlier are revisited and elaborated to accommodate new and more complex reading situations. We have found that by encouraging students to approach these interactive activities in an exploratory and rather playful way, they become more involved and feel more comfortable in sharing their ideas.

Many of the activities can be completed in a cooperative learning group where members problem-solve together. This helps students to try out their thinking and to explicate their ideas. In several chapters we suggest using the "Jigsaw" method in cooperative learning groups. In this method, each group works on one of the case studies in the chapter, and its members become "experts" on that case. After the groups have studied their respective cases, new groups are formed with one expert from each case study. Each expert shares his or her case, and the newly formed group is encouraged to make comparisons among all the cases presented. At each step in the cooperative learning approach, the instructor works with the groups, guiding them toward more complex thinking.

There are several important features of each chapter that should be emphasized:

1. Each chapter begins with a brief introduction to the topic, an explanation of the nature of the interactive activities for understanding the topic, and a list of specific learning objectives.
2. Each introduction is followed by a series of activities, usually between two and four.
3. A description of how to do each activity is provided, with a suggestion to do it alone, with a partner, or in a group.
4. For each activity, students need to use what they already know, not worry about making mistakes, and take risks using their new knowledge.
5. Many activities are followed by cloze activities that help students summarize their new learning. In using these cloze passages, students need to

realize that their knowledge is emerging and developing, so providing exact replacements in the cloze passages is not the goal.

6. After each activity, a follow-up discussion is provided that elaborates the concepts developed in the activity and points the reader in new directions.

It should also be noted that many of the activities in this book can be collected into a personalized handbook for use in the classroom. Students are encouraged to do so, thereby creating their own handbook of reading diagnosis information and practical ideas for reading teaching.

In addition, all of the activities demonstrate certain reading teaching techniques and procedures. For example, various activities use "sorts," features matrices, graphic organizers, and cloze activities as a means of involving students with the content of reading diagnosis. As students complete these activities, they experience how certain techniques and procedures work when learning new information, thus enhancing their preparation for using them in their own teaching. A glossary is also provided to help students use the terminology of reading diagnosis and teaching accurately and appropriate.

Acknowledgments

We owe a great deal to the preservice teachers in our classes who used preliminary drafts of this book and provided us with feedback about the content and organization of these drafts. We are grateful to the staff at Macmillan Publishing Company, especially Linda Scharp, for her belief in the format of the book; Linda Bayma, for her diligent efforts to produce the text according to this new format; and Carol Driver, for insightful editorial suggestions.

Special thanks are also extended to Lisa Lenhart, who so patiently and creatively contributed to the development and refinement of this book. We also wish to thank our reviewers—Carole L. Bond, Memphis State University; Ralph L. Brown, Midwestern State University; Gerald J. Calais, McNeese State University; Nancy E. Clements, Ball State University; Martha Combs, University of Nevada, Reno; Mariam Jean Dreher, University of Maryland; Mary Anne Hall, Georgia State University; Joyce Huizer, Central College; Sondra Lettrich, Seton Hill College; and Leslie A. Patterson, Sam Houston State University—for their perceptive insights.

Contents

To the Student

aug. 29

Yesterday it was the first day of school. I wasn't nervous infact I was happy. At first I that that I wasn't going to have pals, I'm going to talk about some "Ashley is really helpful. Jacob is nice. Seth is AMAZING. TimE. Listens to every bit of Good information Jennifer is ok.

A second grader's journal entry

Helping children become healthy writers and readers is one of our greatest responsibilities as teachers. It is also filled with a great deal of joy and fun. Through the activities in this book, we attempt to develop your knowledge, skill, and thoughtfulness so that you might assume this responsibility with confidence; we also want you to enjoy yourself while doing so. Like the second grader, we hope you are not nervous and that you have some pals. And we definitely encourage you to emulate Tim E., who "listens to every bit of good information."

PART ONE

Fundamentals of Reading Diagnosis

art One of this book presents the fundamentals of reading diagnosis. These fundamentals include (1) a sound understanding of the reading process and of literacy development, (2) familiarity with the process of reading diagnosis and the critical thinking it requires, and (3) practical knowledge of the assessment tools and procedures used in reading diagnosis. A variety of interactive activities are included to introduce you to the basic concepts and skills associated with each of these areas and to provide you with interesting opportunities to explore them. Although our primary aim is to present content that enhances your ability to provide appropriate and effective reading instruction, we also try to demonstrate specific classroom instructional techniques that you can use in your own teaching. In addition, this text provides opportunities to consolidate what you are learning into various resources for your personal use.

In general, two themes are emphasized in Part One of this book. One of these themes is that reading diagnosis is a problem-solving process that relies on knowledgeable teachers making informed decisions. We believe that teachers have a responsibility to become, and to continue to be, informed if they are to effectively diagnose and enhance children's reading behavior and growth. The other theme is that the purpose of reading diagnosis is to improve instruction. This implies that teachers consciously engage in diagnostic activity to make ongoing instructional adjustments and changes. Reading diagnosis is not a once- or twice-a-year activity, nor is it this test or that; it is a dynamic activity that can make reading a satisfying and enjoyable experience for children and teachers alike.

With these ideas in mind, we invite you to participate in several activities that explore and examine the fundamentals of reading diagnosis. Through them you will begin to develop the understandings and skills needed to use reading diagnosis productively in your own teaching.

1

CHAPTER ONE

Foundations

So many instructional methods have been tried, and so many succeed (in some instances at least) ... new ones are unlikely to provide any great gains. What will make a difference is an understanding of the reading process.
—Frank Smith

Educators have spent many years trying to discover *the* method for teaching people to read. Somewhat like the story of the blind men and the elephant—where each man proclaimed his "vision" of the elephant to be the "right" one—different groups at various times claim that they have discovered the *right* method for reading instruction. The flaw in this approach to reading instruction is the belief that success is somehow inherent in the method. We know from research and experience that instructional success is achieved by people, not methods. It is not the basal method, the language-experience approach, nor the whole-language approach that accomplishes learning, per se. Instead, it is how teachers use these ideas and techniques in the teaching of reading that allow students to succeed.

As Frank Smith (1978) suggests, it is informed teachers who make the difference in reading instruction. They understand how children learn and how they develop as readers. They have a firm grasp of the reading process and of the strategies readers use to construct meaning from print. Based on this knowledge, informed teachers make instructional decisions that ultimately influence how children learn through reading. The depth of their knowledge, and subsequently the quality of their decision making, is important in all reading instruction, but it is especially crucial in those situations that involve readers at risk.

As a reading teacher who will make a difference in children's reading achievement, it is useful to explore and extend your own knowledge base, examining how reading occurs and how it develops. Furthermore, it is helpful to reflect on your own beliefs about reading, since these exert a powerful influence on your teaching behaviors. Your understanding of the reading process and of reading development, as well as your own beliefs, form the foundations of the instructional decisions you will inevitably make. Becoming aware of these foundations is a first step in understanding your own knowledge base and in developing that base as an informed teacher of reading.

In the following pages we provide a set of activities that will permit you to examine your own knowledge base about reading. The activities are what is often referred to as "hands-on." That is, they are interactive, requiring your active participation with materials and with others. They are organized in a way that will allow you to use what you already know, while facilitating your discovery of new concepts. In short, you will learn by doing.

There are three main ideas or concepts developed in this set of activities. One of these is that reading is a problem-solving process that includes predicting, confirming, and integrating behaviors. In other words, readers approach print in many of the same ways that they approach other "unknowns" in their lives. They make guesses about it, using what they know. They check their guesses, determining if their guesses make sense or not by confirming them with their own experiences and the print itself. Then they integrate what new information they obtain into their existing knowledge base, thereby expanding what they know. Through repeated use of this process, individuals come to use reading as one means of learning.

Another concept the activities develop is that there are **milestones,** or significant points, in children's literacy development. Born into a literacy-based culture, children strive to make sense out of print from an early age. Through repeated encounters with books, environmental print, and shared reading, they acquire knowledge about the functions and features of written language, deriving basic concepts that support formal literacy instruction. As a teacher of reading, it is important for you to recognize the significant points in children's development of these basic concepts.

Finally, the last activity points out that being aware of your own beliefs about reading instruction is extremely important. In articulating what these beliefs are, you begin to link what you know with what you do, developing your skill as a reflective teacher.

To explore these concepts, you will do three things:

1. Conduct a series of experiments about the reading process;
2. Examine and organize actual samples of children's reading and writing, paying attention to what children can do at different ages; and
3. Generate a list of teaching principles that reflect your current beliefs about reading instruction.

Before you begin, we would like to share a few insights about "discovery" learning that we have gleaned over the years. First and above all, be patient; realize that there are no right answers. Second, use what you already know to make guesses and to initiate the problem-solving process. And, finally, risk sharing what you discover. It is through self-expression that your own learning is manifested.

ACTIVITY 1.1

A cloze procedure is a technique in which words are selectively deleted from a passage and the reader is required to fill in the blanks to construct meaning from the passage.

Revisiting the Reading Process

(*Note:* Do this activity on your own.)

What to Do: In this activity, you will examine the reading process by conducting three reading experiments. As you complete each experiment, draw a conclusion about how reading occurs. A cloze procedure has been provided to aid you in drawing a conclusion based on the experiment.

The following procedure should be used for each experiment:

1. Read the selection.
2. Jot notes in response to the questions that follow the selection.
3. Draw a conclusion, based on your experience, about reading as a process.
4. Write your conclusion, using the cloze passage as an organizer for your thinking.

Experiment 1:
Determining the Language Systems Readers Use

Selection: *The Kingdom of Kay Oss**

Once in the land of Serenity there ruled a king called Kay Oss. The king wanted to be liked by all his people. So one day thx bxnxvolxnt dxspot dxcidxd that no onx in thx country would bx rxsponsiblx for anything. Zll of thx workxrs rxstxd from thxir dzily lxbors. ''Blxss Kzy Oss,'' thxy xxclzimxd.

Now thx lzw mzkxrs wxrx vxry wvsx. But zs wvsx zs thxy wxrx, thxy dxcvdxd thzt thx bxst form of govxrnmxnt wzs nonx zt zll.

Zs tvmx wxnt qn, thx kvngdqm og Kxy Oss bxgzn tq splvt zt thx sxzms znd vt lqqkxd thvs: Bcx dqufhghj klzm nqxp qqt rqst vqxwxxz bqxc dqf ghzj kqlxmnxp. (p. 14)

Questions

What is the selection about?

Why do you think you are able to read it?

What did you do to ''figure out'' the story?

*From CONTENT AREA READING, 3e, by Richard T. Vacca and Jo Anne L. Vacca. Copyright © 1989, 1986 by Richard T. Vacca and Jo Anne L. Vacca. Reprinted by permission of Harper Collins Publishers.

Conclusion

Readers use four language systems to assist them in constructing meaning from print. One of these systems is called the s__man_____ , or meaning, system; sometimes we refer to this more broadly as "using the con_____ ." Another system is the syn_____tic system, or determining how a language is put together. Use of this system reflects our understanding of the gr_____ of a language. A third system we use is the grapho_____ system. Here we demonstrate our knowledge about the relationships between sounds, or pho_____ , and the symbols, or gra_____ , we use to represent them. The fourth system is termed the prag_____tic system. It reveals what we know about different situations in which written language may be used, and the formats that typically accompany such use, for example, a list format for a class roster. Readers rely on all these systems as tools for constructing meaning from print.

Experiment 2:
Determining the Value of Background Knowledge

Selection: *The Stone Foxes* (author unknown)

> I was lookin' over this audience and I see nothin' but stone foxes. I thought to myself, as soon as the eagle flies, I'm gonna go out and rent me a hog or maybe a duce-and-a-quarter, I'm not sure. Then I wanna find the honcho of this organization to let him know I'm gonna lay dead 'cause I'm goin with may hog and stone fox to the killin' floor.

Questions

What is this selection about?

Are you able to read all the words?

If you can read all the words, why are you having trouble constructing meaning?

What do you need to be able to construct meaning?

Conclusion

What we bring to a reading experience makes a difference in whether or not we are able to construct meaning with the print. Our background knowledge, or sche____ta, provides connections which frame and integrate text information so that it makes sense. In other words, what you get from reading is not so much what you see on the page; it is what you can _____ng to the print.

Experiment 3:
Determining Behaviors Readers Use

Selection: *The Indian Boys* (author unknown)

> The boys' arrows were nearly gone so they sat down on the grass and stopped hunting. Over at the edge of the wood they saw Henry making a bow to a small girl who was coming down the road. She had tears in her dress and tears in her eyes. She gave Henry a note which he brought to the group of young hunters. Read to the boys, it caused great excitement. After a minute, but rapid examination of their weapons they ran down to the valley. Does were standing on the edge of the lake, making an excellent target.

Questions

What did you do as a reader during your reading of this passage?

What did you do when things didn't make sense?

Conclusion

Based on this experience, it appears that reading is largely a matter of making guesses or pre_____ , using our sche_____ and our language syst_____ . We check or con_____m our guesses by using text cues and context as sources of information. If things don't make sense, we stop, go back, and fix our initial p_____ . As this process of p_____ing and c_____ing proceeds, we make connections between what we know and what we are reading. In other words, we begin to in____gr_____ the text information with our existing know_____ . By linking what we are reading with what we already know, reading becomes a constructive process. That is, we actually learn through reading. Hence, reading is a process of making p_____ and

c_____ them, while in_____ the printed
information with what we already know.

**FOLLOW-UP
DISCUSSION**

Reflect for a moment about the conclusions you drew from the experiments. In experiment 1, for example, you noted that readers use multiple cueing systems to process written language, while in experiment 2, you observed the importance of what readers *bring* to a printed selection. Experiment 3 helped you recognize the process of reading: making predictions, confirming them, and integrating the text with existing knowledge. As you reconsider these conclusions, think about any generalizations that seem to describe the relationships between them.

One generalization that may have jumped out at you is that reading seems to be a search for meaning. The reader's searching is essentially a problem-solving process, involving the integration (or orchestration) of multiple sources of information—the reader's interests, background knowledge, the situation, and the author's text cues.

The psycholinguistic model illustrates how readers interact with print by predicting, confirming, and integrating in reference to the text.

Figure 1.1 provides a model to help you visualize reading as a problem-solving process. This model is referred to as the **psycholinguistic model** of the reading process, because it attempts to display *how* readers interact with print (Goodman & Burke, 1980).

Examine the model. Notice how print is essentially a medium (or symbol system) shared between two people: the author and the reader. Each contributes to the construction of meaning which results from their interaction. Each individual brings systems of language, schemata, interests, and attitudes to the occasion. Since the author is not physically present, the reader must "carry the conversation," so to speak. The reader actively participates through a dynamic process of predicting, confirming, and integrating, using the textual cues provided by the author as well as her own psycholinguistic resources to construct a meaningful message (Brown, 1985).

As you might suspect, a number of things can go wrong throughout this exchange. For example, the reader may lack background knowledge and therefore miss subtleties shared by the author; he simply is unable to make many connections. Or the reader may fail to confirm her predictions with the actual text and may misread too much of it, misinterpreting the author's message.

Our primary aim as classroom teachers should be to assist all children in their efforts to gain control of the reading process as they learn to use it as a means of constructing meaning with the author's printed message. To do this, we must deliberately plan instruction through which we can engage children in activities and strategies that promote predicting, confirming, and integrating behaviors.

With children at risk in reading, in particular, we need to discover what may be stumbling blocks preventing adequate control of the reading process. For some, an unwillingness to risk "guessing" (or predicting) may stand in the way, shortcir-

FIGURE 1.1
Psycholinguistic model of the
reading process

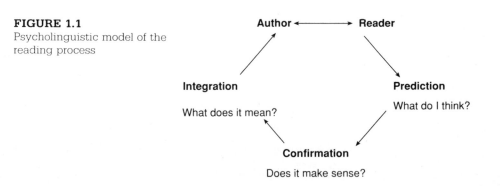

cuiting the entire reading process. For others, failure to confirm may block success, resulting in faulty meaning construction. Still others may have difficulty integrating the total experience into their mental lives, perceiving reading as something to "get done" and then leave behind. In any case, the consequence is a dissatisfying reading experience.

When children have too many unpleasant reading experiences, they start to avoid reading, and the more they avoid it, the less control they have over it. In the end, they cannot use reading effectively as a medium for learning. As a classroom teacher, you must recognize any stumbling blocks in the reading process and then plan ways to assist the reader in removing them.

Thus, your need to understand the reading process is twofold: (1) to make effective instructional plans that will consistently engage children in predicting, confirming, and integrating behaviors, and (2) to sensitively observe reader behaviors to help recognize what may be stumbling blocks for some children. Keep the graphic of the psycholinguistic model as a reference tool; it is one foundation for making decisions about reading instruction.

For now, we will set the process of reading aside, turning next to the fascinating topic of literacy development and how children grow as readers. In the next activity, you will need to rely on your powers of observation as you study samples of children's reading and writing behavior to determine patterns in their literacy growth. As a result of your examination, you will become aware of patterns that broadly characterize literacy development.

ACTIVITY 1.2   **Observing Patterns of Literacy Growth**
(*Note:* Try this activity with a partner or a small group.)

What to Do First: Although there are no reliable developmental milestones applicable to every child's literacy growth, there are patterns in early reading and writing that seem to cut across groups of children. In this activity, you will search for these patterns. You will begin by studying a number of literacy behavior samples gathered from children of different ages. Following your organization of them, you will examine each sample closely, listing your observations. Based on your observations, you will be able to detect some general patterns in children's literacy development. Follow these steps:

1. Clip apart the literacy samples provided in Figure 1.2 on pages 11 to 14. Read the information on the back of each sample.
2. After studying the samples, sort the pictures and transcripts into the following age groups: 0–2 years, 3–5 years, 6–8 years, 9–12+ years.
3. Then match a writing sample to each age grouping.

Arrange your literacy samples in a format similar to the following:

	Picture	*Transcript*	*Writing*
0–2 years			
3–5 years			
6–8 years			
9–12+ years			

What to Do Next: Study the samples carefully. Reread the information on the back of each for additional data. Before going on, take a few moments to jot down a few observations based on the pictures, transcripts, and writing samples. Use the following space or a separate piece of paper to record your ideas.

Observations

Together, let's make some observations based on the literacy samples. First, look at the pictures of the children reading and examine the oral reading transcripts. Did you notice that in the 0–2 age range, the 6-month-old baby can hold a book, and the 19-month-old can turn pages, pointing to pictures in a book? He even "reads" OOOOO on the last page.

FIGURE 1.2
Literacy samples

aprail 11

I stayed for lunch
today. When I get
home I'm going
to play out side
with my freinds.
We made a spey
club. I'm on
a baseball team
called to pun.

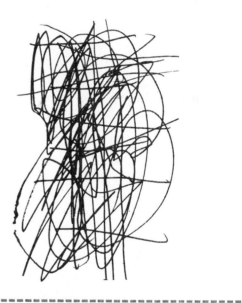

FIGURE 1.2 (continued)

In this picture, the older boy, age 8, is reading to his brother, age 4. As a developing reader, big brother is anxious to share his growing ability to construct meaning with print. Obviously the two are experiencing terror and glee as they read hair-raising stories in *Scared Stiff*.

This child wrote a short piece about school and play activities. Observe in particular the spelling development. Consider also the child's sense of audience, use of mechanics, and punctuation.

This represents a 2-year-old's attempt to jot down a note to a friend. Pay particular attention to the features of the scribble, e.g., its display.

In this picture, the baby is about 6 months old. She is holding a storybook upside down. Observe how she uses her hands *and* her feet to hold the book.

In this scene, mother and child are sharing an ABC book together. The child is pointing and naming pictures while matching them to the ABCs. The mother assists the child in her attempts to relate picture with letter name or sound, as in A is for apple.

This girl is approximately 12 years old. She is silently reading the novel, *Julie of the Wolves,* by Jean Craighead George. Note that she is reading alone and seemingly with pleasure.

Text

Here go the kittens with a fishing rod, a red basket and a pail.
This kitten goes to the pond to catch a fish.
But here come two ducks. They say, "Quack, quack! This pond is ours. Run away, kitten!"
The frightened kitten runs so fast that he falls into the pond.
The little fish laughs.

Re-enactment

The kitten goes to the pond for a — fish.

But some two ducks come. And they say, "This is *my* pond. Run away kitten." So he runs fast and falls in the pond. And the fish laughed.

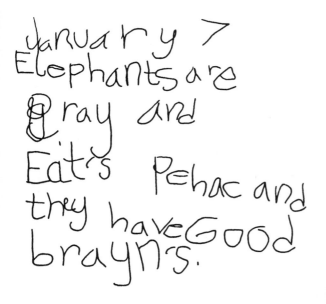

January 7
Elephants are
gray and
Eat's Pehac and
they have Good
brayns.

Steven Retells Bears in the Night *(Berenstain & Berenstain, 1971)*

Story: Bears investigate a sound in the night by creeping out of bed, down a tree, and up a hill.

Steven: (points to moon)	TEXT: IN BED
moon	Illustration: Seven bears in bed. Open window with a crescent moon. A lighted lantern hangs on the wall.
(points to lantern)	
i-eet	
(turns page, points to moon)	Illustration: One bear out of bed, otherwise similar to previous page.
moon	
(points to lantern)	
i-eet	
(turns several pages rapidly, gazes at picture for several seconds)	Illustration: Bear going up hill with lantern in hand. Moon in sky. Owl at the top of hill.
(turns page)	Illustration: The word "WHOOOOO," an owl, and four frightened bears jumping up.
(shakes head, points at owl)	
OOOOOOOOOOO	

Steven

ZTOHAEOE

Owney, the Traveling Dog

It was a cold, snowy evening, but the streets of Albany, N.Y., were crowded with carriages drawn by fine horses. Women in long skirts looked into bright store windows. Men smiled and nodded to one another and called, "Merry Christmas."

Through the lines of carriages came the post office wagon. It was bringing large sacks of mail from the railroad station to the post office.

Even that speed was almost too much for the puppy under the wagon.

He was a very small brown puppy, and he had to run to keep up with the horses. This place, under the wagon, was safe. It was the only safety the puppy had found from the dangers of the city streets. And the wagon kept the snow off him, though he was already so cold and wet it hardly mattered.

⊘ = omission

Food for Birds

"See the small birds," said Jim. "They are looking in the snow. They want food."

"The snow is deep," said Meg. "They cannot find food." Jim said, "Let's help them."

"Yes," said Meg. "We can get bread for them."

Jim and Meg ran home. They asked Mother for bread. Mother gave bread to them. Then they ran to find the birds.

"There are the birds," said Meg. "Give them the bread."

Jim put the bread on the snow.

Meg said, "Look at the birds! They are eating the bread."

"They are happy now," said Jim. "They are fat and happy."

Note. "Owney, the Traveling Dog" from Garrard Publishing, Dallas, TX. "Steven Retells *Bears in the Night*" from Lea M. McGee and Donald J. Richgels, *Literacy's Beginnings: Supporting Young Readers and Writers.* Copyright © 1990 by Allyn and Bacon. Reprinted with permission. "Food for Birds" from Johns, *Basic Reading Inventory Pre-Primer–Grade Eight.* Copyright 1991. Reprinted with permission of Kendall/Hunt Publishing Company.

13

FIGURE 1.2 (continued)

This is Steven's attempt to write an important message: "Stay out of here." What do you notice about the correspondence between the message and the print Steven used? (Note: An adult wrote Steven's name on the paper.)

This is a transcription of a young 4-year-old's attempt to read a picture storybook. Notice the similarities and differences between what the child says and what is in the text.

This is a transcription of a beginning fourth grader's oral reading. The circle around specific words indicates that the child omitted that word while reading. Read as the reader read the piece to obtain a sense of how he processes print and of his overall control of the reading process.

In this writing sample, a 7-year-old conveys some information about elephants. What do you notice about the print, e.g., format, placement, and spelling development?

This is a transcription of a second grader's oral reading. The following coding scheme was used:

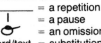

= a repetition
= a pause
= an omission
word/text = substitution

Try to read the selection as the second grader read it to gain some sense of how she reads. Observe her ability to process print and her control of the overall reading process.

This is an example of a very young child engaged in storybook reading at bedtime. Pay close attention to what the child can do, e.g., turn pages. What does the child seem to already know about books and print?

By the age of four, a youngster talk-reads the kitten story, providing a fairly good rendition of the actual text, while the young girl with her mother is beginning to identify alphabet letters, pointing to them and calling them by name.

In the reading transcript of the 7½-year-old, "Food for Birds," we observe the young child's increasing ability to read actual words, processing ever more accurately the print on the page. The picture of the two boys reading *Scared Stiff* further illustrates children's increasing control over print, using it as a source of pleasure and fright.

Finally, in the "Owney" passage, we see a fluent reader at work, processing print and meaning with ease. Likewise, the girl reading to herself demonstrates the mature reader's ability to construct meaning with text in an almost invisible way.

What about the writing samples you sorted into the different age ranges? How does writing seem to start? Did you observe that actual letters seem to appear around age 4, just when children seem to be noticing alphabet letters in books?

Look at the 7-year-old's piece about elephants. Did you notice her invented spelling of "brayns" for "brains?" Apparently, as children mature they experiment with many ways of writing words, striving to understand how written language works. By the age of 9½, children appear to have considerable control of writing as a medium of expression, as the writing sample suggests.

What to Do Last:　The obvious literacy accomplishments that children make at certain ages represent significant points in their literacy development. Taken together, these points suggest a pattern of early reading and writing.

With your partner, record the significant points in reading and writing that you observed in the samples for each age range. Write them down in a chart form something like that illustrated in Figure 1.3. To spark your thinking, a few points have been provided for you.

FIGURE 1.3
Significant points in literacy development

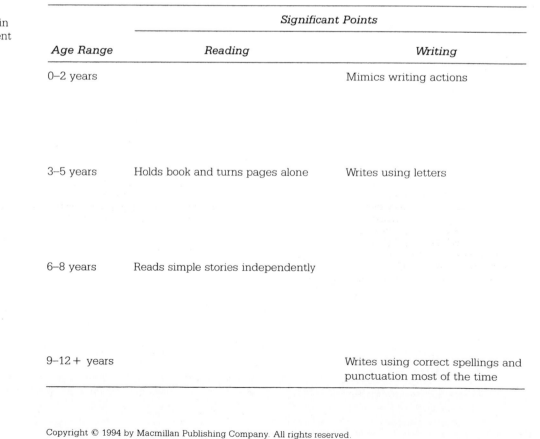

	Significant Points	
Age Range	Reading	Writing
0–2 years		Mimics writing actions
3–5 years	Holds book and turns pages alone	Writes using letters
6–8 years	Reads simple stories independently	
9–12 + years		Writes using correct spellings and punctuation most of the time

FOLLOW-UP DISCUSSION

Take a moment to study the patterns you have observed. As you worked through this activity, you learned that children strive to make sense with print, starting from a very early age. Their development can be marked by milestones or significant points along the way. Describing these milestones in your own words will help you interpret reading and writing behaviors of the children you teach. We recommend matching your significant points with the literacy samples and then using the samples and your descriptions to begin your own diagnostic practices book. Such a resource will help you interpret reading behaviors throughout this text and in your teaching. Use Figure 1.4 to compare your findings to those determined by another pair of students.

As you examine children's emerging literacy achievements, do you note any patterns that seem to characterize children's literacy development overall? For example, did you notice that children seem to move from a vague understanding of what literacy is all about to a more precise (and accurate) understanding? Of course they do! Just as there are patterns organizing the design of a piece of cloth or a work of art, there are overarching patterns in literacy development. Three such patterns in particular are especially apparent. In the following discussion, we briefly describe each pattern and indicate educators who discuss it in greater depth. You may choose to further your understanding by reading their work. As you read, picture in your mind how your recent observations of the samples fit into each of these patterns.

Pattern 1:
From Global Notions and Actions
to Specific Notions and Actions
(Bissex, 1980; Piaget, 1962)

Recall the picture of the 6-month-old baby holding a book. Although you may strongly suspect she is not really reading, from the baby's point of view, she is.

Initial concepts about literacy are necessarily global in nature, focusing on the *most apparent* aspects of reading and writing. After all, it's hard to come to know something you cannot see, touch, and manipulate. To the very young child, holding a book *is* reading, since that is the most evident of all readers' actions. Holding a pencil and marking on paper (or anything else) is writing, because that is what writers appear to do.

Pattern 1: Children's understanding of reading becomes increasingly more specific.

Through multiple encounters with print—bedtime stories, environmental print, play, literacy conversations with others, schooling—young children come to realize that there's more to reading and writing than meets the eye. They discover that there is more happening than just holding a book or a pencil. They become increasingly aware of all the reader or writer needs to know and do in his head when using print as a medium for communication. Put quite simply, children get smarter about how literacy works, and their earlier naive views of reading and writing give way to more informed ones.

FIGURE 1.4
Student sample of observations of significant points in literacy development

| Age Range | Significant Points | |
	Reading	Writing
0–2 years	Pretends to read own book	Scribbles
3–5 years	Memorizes favorite book Reads environmental print	Prephonemic writing
6–8 years	A beginning reader Knows many more sight words	Invented spellings
9–12+ years	Reads independently	Transitional and conventional writing

Pattern 2:
From Invention to Convention
(Clay, 1967; Downing, 1979; Ferreiro & Teberosky, 1982; Piaget, 1972)

This pattern is probably the most noticeable in young children's writing. Take another look at the writing samples across the age groupings. Observe how children's written language attempts (or inventions) advance toward more conventional forms.

Through their experimentation, children gain more and more control over the formation of the written marks used in English. They also develop concepts about orientation (left to right; top to bottom), punctuation, and language units, such as words, sentences, and so on. Children need many opportunities for experimentation and invention with written language to achieve convention consistently.

Invention is also evident in children's early reading attempts. Elizabeth Sulzby (1985) describes this quite clearly in her classification scheme for children's emergent reading of storybooks. When children "read by looking" and "form oral stories," or "talk-read," they reinvent the story, using pictures, not print, as a guide. With increasing word awareness and knowledge, children begin to rely more on the printed forms as cues. When this occurs, they more closely approximate the author's words instead of their own version of the story.

John Downing (1979) proposes that these "inventive" attempts characterize the learning-to-read process. He suggests that this process consists of "rediscovering" the functions and rules of written language. Invented spellings and "talk-reading" favorite storybooks may actually represent children's efforts to re-create the English writing system!

Pattern 2: Through experimentation and discovery, children invent and reinvent theories about written language, which gradually become more conventional.

Pattern 3:
From External Control of Meaning Construction
to Self-Control of Meaning Construction
(Holdaway, 1979; Rogoff, 1989; Vygotsky, 1962)

Look at the pictures accompanying the age groupings again. Notice that in many of the pictures, there is another person present, assisting the reader/writer.

Although we tend to view reading and writing as solitary, private activities, they are not. Literacy begins and ends in the company of others. A child enters a life of literacy invited and assisted by one more informed. This literacy "teacher" (parent, sibling, peer, or any other more informed individual) demonstrates how meaning is constructed with print. The bedtime story is an excellent example of such "teaching"; it is purposeful, meaningful, and enjoyable. As a result of many literacy experiences like the bedtime story, the child assumes increasing responsibility for the construction of meaning until she is "in charge."

Lauren Resnick (1990) refers to learning literacy in this way as "apprenticeship." It involves being coached while doing, with decreasing degrees of support from the "master." In a literacy-intensive society there are many situations where children can be "apprenticed" into literacy. Reading with peers, playing board games, dining out, and storybook reading are just a few examples. Do not underestimate the importance of these literacy events that occur outside the school doors; they, too, assist children in gaining control of reading as a meaning-making activity.

Pattern 3: Children are "apprenticed" into literacy by those more informed, and gradually assume responsibility for constructing meaning with print.

We hope you find these patterns useful for organizing your growing knowledge about literacy development. Before you move on to the next activity, cross-check the significant points you noted in the literacy samples with those provided in the timeline of Philip Tyler's literacy growth (Figure 1.5). Keep Figure 1.5 and your own chart as reference tools. Both provide a foundation for determining developmental appropriateness in instructional planning.

FIGURE 1.5
Philip Tyler's literacy development

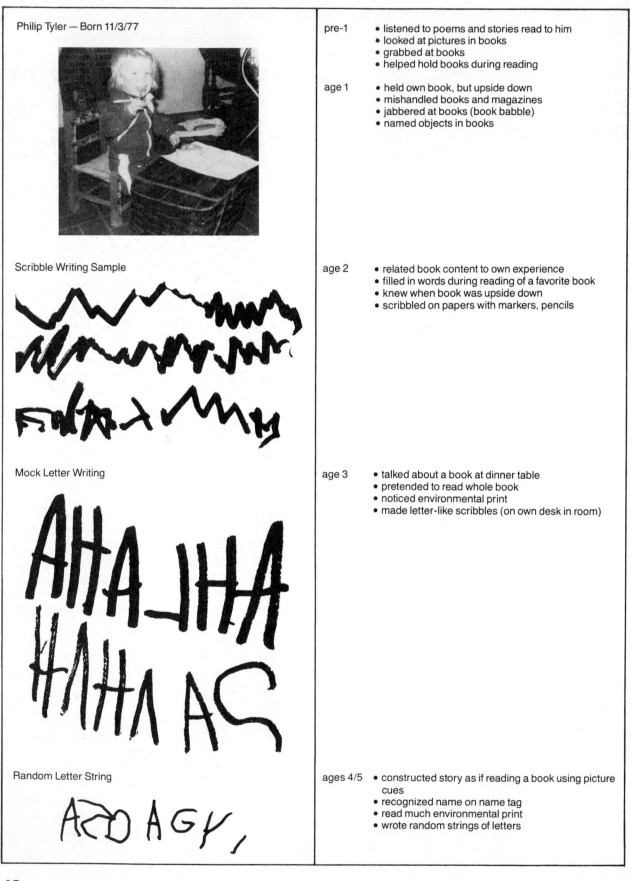

Philip Tyler — Born 11/3/77

Scribble Writing Sample

Mock Letter Writing

Random Letter String

pre-1
- listened to poems and stories read to him
- looked at pictures in books
- grabbed at books
- helped hold books during reading

age 1
- held own book, but upside down
- mishandled books and magazines
- jabbered at books (book babble)
- named objects in books

age 2
- related book content to own experience
- filled in words during reading of a favorite book
- knew when book was upside down
- scribbled on papers with markers, pencils

age 3
- talked about a book at dinner table
- pretended to read whole book
- noticed environmental print
- made letter-like scribbles (on own desk in room)

ages 4/5
- constructed story as if reading a book using picture cues
- recognized name on name tag
- read much environmental print
- wrote random strings of letters

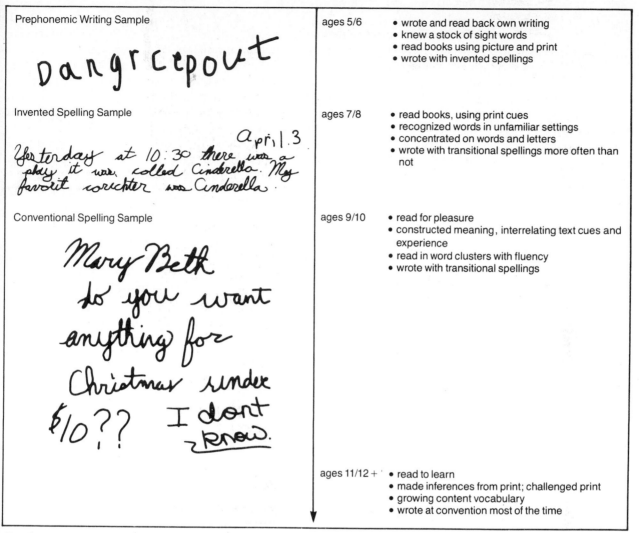

Prephonemic Writing Sample	ages 5/6	• wrote and read back own writing • knew a stock of sight words • read books using picture and print • wrote with invented spellings
Dangrcepout		
Invented Spelling Sample	ages 7/8	• read books, using print cues • recognized words in unfamiliar settings • concentrated on words and letters • wrote with transitional spellings more often than not
April 3 Yesterday at 10:30 there was a play it was called Cinderella. My favorit worichter was Cinderella.		
Conventional Spelling Sample	ages 9/10	• read for pleasure • constructed meaning, interrelating text cues and experience • read in word clusters with fluency • wrote with transitional spellings
Mary Beth do you want anything for Christmas under $10?? I dont know.		
	ages 11/12 +	• read to learn • made inferences from print; challenged print • growing content vocabulary • wrote at convention most of the time

See also:

Schickedanz, J. (1986). *More than the ABCs: The early stages of reading and writing.* Washington, DC: National Association for the Education of Young Children.

Cochrane, O., Cochrane, D., Scalena, S., & Buchanen, E. (1984). *Reading, writing and caring.* New York: Richard Owen.

Weaver, C. (1988). *Reading process and practice: From socio-psycholinguistics to whole language* (pp. 206–207). Portsmouth, NH: Heinemann.

Before we close our exploration of the foundations of diagnosis, we need to examine one other dimension: your personal ideas about literacy teaching and learning. These beliefs exert a powerful influence on how your understandings are translated into teaching actions. Hence, in our final activity, we ask you to look inward, determining what ideas are at the core of your approach to literacy teaching.

ACTIVITY 1.3   ## Generating Literacy Teaching Principles

(*Note:* Do this activity on your own.)

What to Do: Recall a particular time recently when you were in the role of teacher. Perhaps you were working with a group of children in a classroom, reading to a small group, or helping another teacher with an activity. Bring this incident vividly to mind and reflect on it for a moment, considering what you believed about your role in the situation. Were you trying to make sure children listened attentively or demonstrating a particular task or skill? Were you eliciting their opinions or attempting to follow their lead in a discussion?

Reflecting on, or rethinking, the teaching we do provides an excellent opportunity to examine our own beliefs about teaching and learning. Why bother?, you may be wondering. One important reason is that our beliefs have a great influence on what we do. Our awareness of them makes it easier for us to reexamine them periodically, especially when confronted with new and compelling information. Such reexamination, in turn, aids us in remaining open to change in our teaching practices, restructuring them to meet new challenges and conditions.

In this activity you will have an opportunity to reflect on your experiences as a literacy teacher so far, and to synthesize your thoughts into a set of literacy teaching beliefs. Based on your past and current literacy teaching experiences, as well as those in this chapter, develop at least five principles which you think summarize your beliefs about literacy teaching. For example, you may feel that children's interests are key when planning reading experiences. When you have collected your thoughts, write them in the space provided.

Principles of Literacy Teaching

I believe literacy teaching . . .

FOLLOW-UP DISCUSSION

Principles of literacy teaching guide the practice of literacy teaching.

"We can believe what we choose [but] we are answerable for what we choose to believe." Cardinal Newman (1848) makes an excellent point and provides a primary reason for stating principles that consolidate your beliefs about literacy teaching and your understandings of reading development and processes. What you believe guides your instructional preferences and choices. In other words, what you believe influences what you do. It is your professional responsibility to know what guides you in your teaching so that you are able to explain what you do.

Brian Cambourne (1990), for example, identified two principles that reflect his beliefs about literacy teaching:

1. The literacy we teach in schools should be durable, and
2. Learning to be literate should be as uncomplicated and barrier-free as possible.

Like Cambourne, stating the principles that synthesize your beliefs and understandings at any given point in time is one way of organizing your thinking. Your principles become statements that express your own ideas about literacy teaching and learning.

Summary

Through the activities in this chapter, you examined and reviewed the foundations of reading diagnosis. You revisited the reading process, experiencing the predicting, confirming, and integrating behaviors that characterize this dynamic activity. You also investigated how literacy develops, observing a number of literacy samples and noting patterns of development. Finally, you looked at your own beliefs about literacy teaching, recognizing the necessity for periodic reflection about them.

As a result of engaging in the activities, you constructed three reference tools for use in the diagnostic teaching of reading: a model of the reading process, a chart showing patterns of literacy development, and a written collection of literacy teaching principles reflective of your own beliefs. These tools illustrate the foundations of reading diagnosis and can help you organize your growing knowledge base about literacy acquisition and learning.

Further Reading

Goodman, K. (1989). *What's whole in whole language.* Ontario, Canada: Scholastic. Provides a basic and simple overview of the whole-language perspective.

Hall, N. (1987). *The emergence of literacy.* Portsmouth, NH: Heinemann. Discusses the concept of emergent literacy and how children make sense of print before they begin school.

Mason, J. (1989). *Reading and writing connections.* Boston: Allyn & Bacon. Includes a collection of articles by early literacy experts, tracing the development of reading and writing and describing classroom contexts that support early literacy.

Meek, M. (1982). *Learning to read.* London: Bodley Head. Explains literacy development from before the age of five through adolescence in a very readable style; an excellent resource for parents.

Newman, J. (1985). *Whole language—theory in use.* Portsmouth, NH: Heinemann. Overviews the psycholinguistic perspective and provides examples of classroom practices.

Teale, W., & Sulzby, E. (1986). *Emergent literacy—writing and reading.* Norwood, NJ: Ablex. Presents eight research articles that articulate the concept of emergent literacy and detail the literacy behaviors indicative of this phase of development.

CHAPTER TWO

The Process of Diagnosis

Diagnosis is nothing more than the application of a straightforward, common sense, problem-solving approach to the study of children who have difficulties in reading.
—Albert Harris and Edward Sipay

Process of diagnosis: The mental activity associated with making decisions about individuals' reading behaviors.

In this chapter, we focus on the **process of diagnosis.** When we use this phrase, we mean the mental activity associated with making decisions about individuals' reading behaviors. **Critical thinking**—the process of taking ideas apart, selecting important aspects, and then reorganizing the ideas to affect action or make a point— is central to the diagnostic process. Critical thinking requires that we use the best of our analytical abilities to understand the reading behaviors of others, and especially of those who are problem readers. Furthermore, the process of diagnosis is **dynamic,** which means that it does not stand still; it is ongoing and continually changing. Diagnosis is an active process in reading instruction, occurring as teachers teach and as learners learn.

Because of these qualities, the process of diagnosis is a demanding one to learn, challenging our mental resources and our teaching skills. Consequently, the interactive activities in this chapter are designed to acquaint you with the thinking that the diagnostic process entails, and to provide you with an opportunity to practice these cognitive behaviors. We begin by comparing the process of diagnosis to the more general process of problem solving, introducing you to the mental activity of theorizing. Following this, we present a model of the diagnostic process, which illustrates the key thinking behaviors we use when engaged in diagnostic teaching. Finally, we involve you in a case study to provide an opportunity for you to practice the critical thinking central to the process of diagnosis.

In many ways, the process of diagnosis resembles the broader one of problem solving—a process we are all familiar with. Small or large, personal or social, we are all busy solving problems. What must I do to pass this course? What topic should I choose for a teaching project? What will I do on Saturday night? and so on.

Theorizing: The mental activity involved in creating a solution to a problem.

The actual thinking we do to solve a problem involves the mental activity of **theorizing.** Essentially we "think up," or invent, a solution to our problem. How do we do this? Let's take a rather humorous children's story, *Henry's Awful Mistake* by Robert Quackenbush (1980), as an example of theorizing.

The main character in this story is Henry the duck, who has a problem. He had asked his friend Clara over for supper, then found an ant in his kitchen while he was preparing the food. Fearing Clara would think his house was dirty, Henry tried to figure out a way to get rid of the ant. Should he use ant spray? No, it may contaminate the food (and harm the environment). Should he smash the ant with a frying pan? "Yes," Henry thought.

23

He tried, but missed. The ant got away and hid in a crack in the wall. Now what? Henry decided to use a hammer to knock a hole in the wall to get at the ant, but he hit a water pipe instead. Obviously, Henry's decision was a mistake because he flooded his kitchen and ruined a romantic supper. But Henry got smarter: The next time he saw the ant, he looked the other way!

Henry's "awful mistake" provides us with a humorous, albeit simplified, version of the mental theorizing we do when solving a problem. Like Henry, we ask ourselves questions, risk guesses, make inferences, and draw conclusions (which sometimes may turn out to be awful mistakes). As mental operations, asking questions, risking guesses, making inferences, and drawing conclusions are thinking behaviors at the core of the diagnostic process.

Let's take another look at theorizing, this time using an example closer to our topic of study—literacy teaching. In the following account, Mr. Lenhart, a third-grade teacher, is engaged in some preliminary theorizing about one of his students, Jamaal. Although abbreviated, the excerpt illustrates the thinking behaviors that characterize theorizing with respect to the diagnostic process.

It is the beginning of the school year, and Mr. Lenhart has introduced daily journal writing to his students. Periodically, he collects the students' journals to observe how students are using written language as a means of personal expression. In particular, Mr. Lenhart notes content, mechanics, and spelling development, using this information to guide his instruction of groups and individuals.

What follows is a description of his "thinking" while reading one of Jamaal's entries, provided in Figure 2.1. A more conventional version of the entry is also provided. For your reference, Geauga Lake is an amusement park in the local area.

"What's this? How well does he use print to express his ideas? Looks like Jamaal will write about his experiences, the Geauga Lake thing and so on. But there's not too much, here. Seems he is aware of a paragraph format, though.

Is he 'sounding his way' through words? Looks like it: here he wrote *luke* for *lucky,* so he is applying some graphophonemic knowledge. Maybe he's in a late letter-name stage of spelling development. He could use some instruction about spelling patterns. And I'll have to try to boost his fluency with writing, as well as his use of detail and an awareness of audience.

Great, he likes football, which could become an area of reading interest that I can use to motivate him. We could possibly expand that to some other sports—even sports figures.

I'll need to encourage him to tell me, through his journal writing, more about playing football with his friends, and use this as one means to increase his

FIGURE 2.1
Jamaal's journal entry

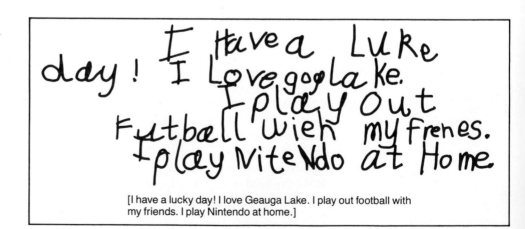

[I have a lucky day! I love Geauga Lake. I play out football with my friends. I play Nintendo at home.]

volume and use of detail. I must also assist him in his spelling development, bringing him increasingly toward convention.''

Notice how Mr. Lenhart examines Jamaal's writing, asking himself questions, risking guesses, making inferences, and drawing conclusions. He is theorizing about Jamaal's literacy development and growth, using those foundations we discussed in Chapter One—knowledge of literacy development, the reading process, and personal beliefs.

Although this excerpt represents only a ''snapshot'' of the diagnostic process, note how common problem-solving behaviors combine with specific understandings of reading and writing to bring about theorizing appropriate to diagnosis. The important consequence of this intense mental activity is instructional decision making. In the end, we want the theorizing we do to be more like that of Mr. Lenhart and less like that of Henry the duck. We want to avoid too many awful mistakes.

At this point, you may note how cognitively complex the process of diagnosis is, how dynamic, and how continuous! Like other processes we strive to gain control of, it takes practice. In the following activities we offer several opportunities for you to practice the process of diagnosis; but realize that this is only a beginning, since diagnosis is a process that develops over time and with experience.

We begin in a general way, bringing to the fore those problem-solving behaviors you already possess. We next compare and contrast problem-solving behaviors, noting likenesses and differences in theorizing styles. Having acquainted you with the process of problem solving in a more general sense, we then introduce you to a model of the diagnostic process. This model provides a visible structure of the ongoing and dynamic theorizing that occurs in diagnostic teaching. It also rightfully directs our work in the remaining chapters, serving as a touchstone for problem solving and a pattern of instructional behavior. To the extent that our work reflects this model, it is likely to be fruitful and effective. Finally, we invite you ''to play with the process,'' providing you with an abbreviated case study for practice. Through your interactions in these activities, you will:

1. reflect on your own theorizing while solving a simple problem;
2. become familiar with a model of the diagnostic process; and
3. develop your diagnostic teaching skills by using a diagnostic process model to examine an excerpt from a case study.

ACTIVITY 2.1   **The Mystery Photo: Theorizing in Action**
(*Note:* Try this activity with a partner.)

What to Do: You may have done this before—looked at a close-up of something and tried to guess what it might be. Actually, this playful activity is an example of theorizing in a nutshell. Let's try this simple ''identification'' exercise, this time for the purpose of exploring the theorizing we do to solve a problem.

Examine the following photo. It is a close-up of a common household object. Can you identify what it is? To solve the mystery, you will need to ask questions, risk guesses, make inferences, and draw a conclusion.

FOLLOW-UP DISCUSSION   The purpose of this activity was to simulate problem solving in a very general and uncomplicated way. As you were trying to solve the mystery of what the photo illustrated, you were using the problem-solving process just as you would in every-day situations.

To solve the mystery, you needed to theorize. And in doing this mental activity, you used certain mental behaviors. For example,

♦ You asked yourself questions like, ''Is this candy?''
♦ You risked some guesses, such as, ''Maybe it's that penny candy.''
♦ You inferred—''But there seem to be ridges, and penny candy is smooth.''
♦ And finally you drew a conclusion—''It's those . . .''

While you were solving the mystery, you probably did not notice these mental behaviors, since they were occurring rapidly as you shuttled back and forth between asking yourself questions, risking guesses, making inferences, and drawing conclusions. Nevertheless, this simple exercise provides you with some sense of how dynamic, continuous, and active the process of problem solving is.

In the next activity we continue our exploration of the problem-solving process, examining more closely the theorizing we do to solve everyday problems. Our familiarity with problem solving in this more general sense will then serve as a springboard for understanding it in relation to reading diagnosis.

ACTIVITY 2.2 **Thinking About Your Own Theorizing**
(*Note:* Try this activity with a partner.)

What to Do: In your mind, retrace the problem solving you did in Activity 2.1. Try to recall each step. What did you do right away? What next? Then what did you do? And what else?

As you recall your own theorizing, in the following space sketch the "route" of your problem solving by illustrating what you did. When you are finished, compare your "theorizing" route with your partner's, noting similarities and differences.

Problem-solving Route

FOLLOW-UP DISCUSSION Since as individuals we prefer to think in our own way, probably no two sketches of our theorizing will be exactly alike. However, despite our differences, there are phases in the theorizing we do when problem solving which are common to us all.

Theorizing begins with looking. Looking gives way to observing more closely. Once we begin to observe attentively, we start to analyze. And in analyzing, we begin to note relationships among parts and between each part and the whole. As we do so, we make connections in an effort to make sense of what we observe. These interpretations prompt conclusions and judgments, which in turn influence our future looking. Although routes for this mental activity may vary, all include these phases.

In Figure 2.2 we have consolidated a number of individual sketches into one general version of the problem-solving process. Take a moment to study it, then compare it to your own sketch. What are the common features between it and yours? What are the distinct differences?

FIGURE 2.2
A model of the problem-solving
process

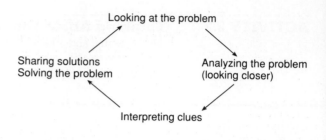

The process of diagnosis is a way of behaving while teaching reading. It involves looking, analyzing, interpreting, making instructional adjustments and rethinking one's own theorizing.

Subtle differences aside, for all of us problem solving is a process—a way of behaving that includes some looking, analyzing, interpreting, and sharing. This process has no clear end point, spiraling on and on throughout a lifetime.

Similarly, diagnosis is also a process—a way of behaving while teaching reading, embedding diagnosis in the ebb and flow of reading instruction. Figure 2.3 illustrates this process of diagnosis, depicting it as one of

◆ observing reading behaviors,
◆ identifying patterns and comparing them to healthy reading processes,
◆ interpreting and judging the quality of reading behaviors,
◆ suggesting instructional adjustments, and
◆ thinking about one's own theorizing overall.

Note the similarities between your own theorizing in Activity 2.1 and the theorizing shown in this model of the diagnostic process. There are many similarities—observing, for instance, as well as making inferences (interpretation), and drawing conclusions (translation).

There are also some important differences. Analysis, for example, involves identifying the attributes of an individual's reading behavior, discerning patterns, and then relating these to a knowledge base, specifically that of reading development and growth. Likewise, the diagnostic model includes a reflection phase where the individual rethinks his or her own theorizing as a whole, becoming sensitive to the coherence and appropriateness of what was observed, what was inferred, and what was translated into instructional action.

In the following paragraphs, we describe more fully the different phases of the diagnostic process as depicted in Figure 2.3 to familiarize you with the kind of theorizing that diagnosis requires. Following this, you will participate in an activity where you use the diagnostic process in a limited way, beginning to link it to the more general theorizing you already do.

Observations   Let's begin with the observation phase of the diagnostic process. **Observation** is the process of examining actual literacy behaviors. Many observations of individuals' reading behaviors begin with questions, such as, Why does Rosa have difficulty reading fluently? or Why does James remember the details of a story but miss the main idea?

FIGURE 2.3
A model of the diagnostic process

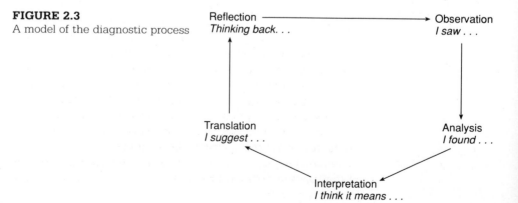

To answer your questions, look closely at the literacy behaviors of the learners you are studying. The answers to these questions become observations. To examine Rosa's reading fluency, you could listen to Rosa read orally, but you should also want to know if she predicts what might happen next. Predicting would help her fluency, as would her familiarity with the topic. In other words, it is important to use **multiple indicators of performance,** which means examining the reading behaviors of individuals by using more than one data source. We cannot be "Johnny one-notes," relying on only one source of information. Like surveyors, we must look at readers' behaviors from different points to obtain a more accurate "fix" as to what they can and cannot do.

To acquaint you with a wide range of sources from which to gather information about individuals' reading behaviors, Chapters Three and Nine describe a number of informal and formal assessment tools. Using a combination of these tools to observe children's reading behaviors provides a means of obtaining multiple indicators of their reading performance.

Multiple indicators of performance: *Examining, from more than one data source, an individual's reading behaviors.*

Analysis Analysis is a mental activity that involves "taking things apart," examining relationships among different parts as well as the relationships of the parts to the whole. In the mystery photo activity, for example, you examined the picture very closely, looking at the different parts, searching for clues that provided information about the whole thing. As you compared the different parts, you began your analysis. You asked yourself how the pieces fit together.

Analyzing reading behaviors is very similar. Here we look closely at reading behaviors, scrutinizing their predicting, confirming, and integrating properties. For example: What is the quality of the reader's predictions? How does she confirm, using textual and contextual cues? What indicates that the reader constructs meaning with print? In Rosa's case, we observe that she isn't predicting, and we also observe that she seldom uses background knowledge. Our analysis put these parts together so we could look at the whole process: Rosa doesn't always predict by using what she knows.

During analysis, we compare our observations with what we know about the reading process and reading development, noting patterns of reading behavior that support the effective use of the reading process, and those that deter it. Clearly our analytic skills rest on a solid understanding of the reading process and literacy development, since we cannot "see" what we do not yet know. In brief, analysis is the detail work of diagnosis, where information about an individual's reading behaviors is processed for the purpose of determining how the reader constructs meaning. In Chapter Three, we will discuss several analytic procedures that help to guide this phase of the diagnostic process, such as miscue analysis and retelling analysis.

Analysis: *The detail work of diagnosis where observations from multiple sources are compared, noting how the reader constructs meaning.*

Interpretation Looking closely and analyzing is not enough to make instructional decisions about reading. As teachers of reading, we need to make sense of what we see with respect to the context in which it occurs. In other words, we need to make the data *meaningful,* considering the individual reader and the situation.

We do this by interpreting, using our knowledge of children and how they learn, of literacy development and the reading process, as well as using the situation and our own instructional experiences and intuition. In general, **interpretation** occurs when we infer and summarize reading strengths and needs, verifying these with our knowledge base. Inevitably we must appraise or judge, along a continuum of developmental appropriateness, the status of what we see. Looking at Rosa's case we find that she is fairly fluent for a second grader (her grade placement) when she reads familiar text. However, she stumbles when she encounters unfamiliar stories in her reader, because she doesn't use her background knowledge to predict what might happen next. She has strengths in calling words, but needs to work on prediction strategies.

Interpretation: *Making information about an individual's reading behaviors meaningful by drawing inferences based on an analysis of the reader's performance, development, and the situation, resulting in a summary of strengths and needs.*

Making interpretations requires thoughtfulness and, ultimately, the ability to make decisions. Both of these activities are challenging and time-consuming. However, without carefully interpreting any information gathered about children's reading behaviors, subsequent instruction may not respond to children's strengths and needs with appropriate intervention techniques. In short, our teaching may "miss the mark." Through the case studies provided in the remaining chapters of this book, we provide you with multiple opportunities to practice interpreting the reading behaviors you have observed and analyzed.

Translation: Sharing interpretations with appropriate audiences and applying them to actual instruction.

Translation   To **translate** is to transfer from one form to another. In reading diagnosis, this includes two activities: One, the findings you derive need to be shared in a meaningful way with those who care about them the most—the readers themselves, their parent(s), and your colleagues; and two, your findings need to be applied to actual instruction. For example, we might suggest to Rosa's mother that Rosa be encouraged to read predictable books to her younger brother, asking him to guess what might happen next. In the classroom, however, you might help Rosa use her background knowledge to make predictions about what she is reading by modeling your own prediction-making processes when reading a story.

Whether we are talking with parents or fellow teachers, we must make adjustments in what we say and how we say it and in what we do and how we do it. For instance, we should strive to limit teaching jargon when talking with parents, but probably not when talking with a colleague. And, too, what we do in the classroom to meet learners' needs is undoubtedly going to be more complex and intensive than what we recommend for home activities. In the ensuing chapters, translation activities are elaborated and described in greater detail.

Reflection: Rethinking and critiquing one's own diagnostic theorizing.

Reflection   The **reflection** phase of the diagnostic process provides an opportunity to distance oneself from the experience, rethinking the theorizing that has occurred and then critiquing it. As instructional adjustments are made, we begin to notice new and different behaviors and to ask new questions, thereby stimulating the continuation of the diagnostic process. At this point, decisions made throughout the process are reconsidered for their soundness, accuracy, and appropriateness, leading to the construction of a rationale for instructional adjustments. It is this rationale that helps teachers know why they teach as they do and facilitates their explanations to others. Consequently, this is a vital phase in the diagnostic process, serving as a monitor to the teacher's own thinking and underpinning the credibility of the overall endeavor. Various aspects of reflection in the diagnostic process and in teaching are elaborated further in Chapter Eight.

Before we leave this chapter, it is important that you experience the process of diagnosis in a more realistic sense. To that end, the final activity involves you in an abbreviated case study, where you will diagnose a few samples of writing behavior. Please keep in mind that the case has been condensed, providing an extremely limited view of an individual's literacy behavior. However, our purpose here is to explore theorizing as it applies to reading diagnosis, acquainting you with a diagnostic process you will apply to a greater degree later in more detailed case studies.

ACTIVITY 2.3   **A Case Study**

(*Note:* Share your results with a small group or a partner.)

What to Do: Recall from the model that the diagnostic process begins with the observation of literacy behaviors. The abbreviated version of the case study in this activity provides observational information that you can analyze, interpret, and translate into instructional suggestions. It also presents an opportunity to reflect on your own theorizing and decision making, stimulating the elaboration and refinement of your personal beliefs about literacy processes.

Read the following abbreviated case study of Gill, an eight-year-old boy in the third grade. Then study the samples of his writing behavior shown in Figure 2.4. The samples were drawn from his daily journal and, therefore, represent unedited drafts.

As you observe, analyze, and interpret information about Gill, translating it into instructional interventions, jot down notes on the figure of the diagnostic process provided in the Questions section of this activity. At some point, look back at your theorizing and record your reflections.

FIGURE 2.4
Gill's journal entries

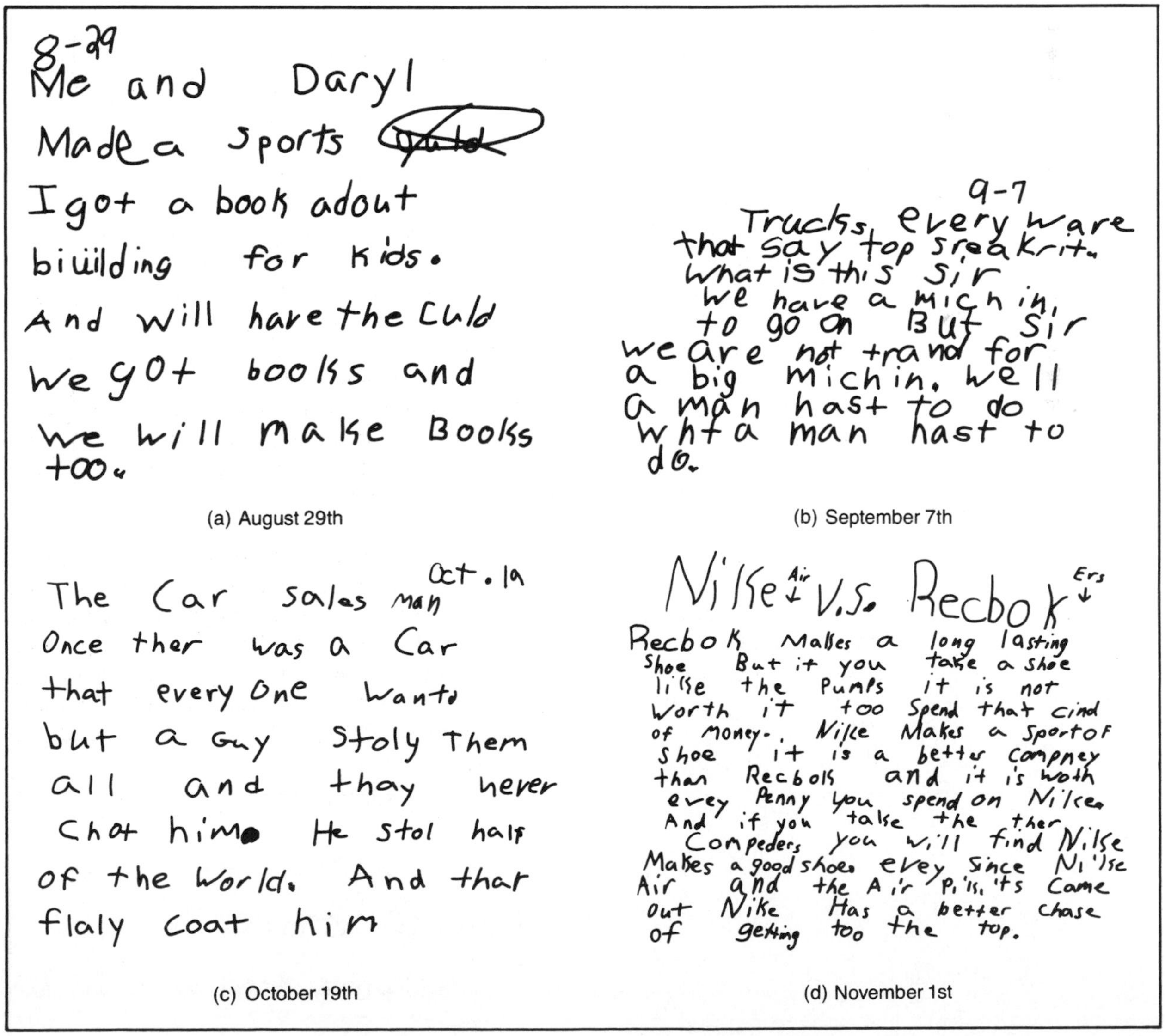

8-29
Me and Daryl
Made a sports ~~Dutch~~
I got a book adout
biuilding for kids.
And will have the Culd
we got boolss and
we will make Boolss
too.

(a) August 29th

9-7
Trucks every ware
that say top sreakrit.
what is this sir
we have a michin,
to go on But sir
we are not trand for
a big michin. well
a man hast to do
wht a man hast to
do.

(b) September 7th

Oct. 19
The Car sales man
Once ther was a Car
that every One Wantd
but a Guy Stoly Them
all and thay never
Chat him. He stol half
of the world. And thar
flaly coat him

(c) October 19th

Nike ± Air V.S. Recbok Ers

Recbok Malses a long lasting
Shoe But if you tare a shoe
lise the Punps it is not
worth it too Spend that cind
of Money. Nilse Makes a sportof
Shoe it is a better Compney
than Recbols and it is woth
evey Penny you spend on Nilse.
And if you talse the ther
Compeders you will find Nilse
Makes a good shoe evey Since Nilse
Air and the Air Pils its Came
out Nike Has a better chase
of getting too the top.

(d) November 1st

Gill is an eight-year-old boy. In his third-grade classroom, a literature-based reading program is used. Currently Gill is reading *Fantastic Mr. Fox* by Roald Dahl (1970), but he is not particularly interested in the story. The writing program includes daily journal writing along with a writing workshop during which the writing process is emphasized.

Although Gill demonstrates above-average intelligence, he barely achieves average scores on third-grade work in comparison with his peers. He does not express a strong interest in reading or writing, claiming that both of these activities are "boring." His favorite activity at school is art.

In general, Gill has difficulty constructing meaning with print. This is indicated by his poor ability to retell selections he has read and his lack of participation in small-group discussions. On an informal reading inventory, his reading levels were as follows:

Independent reading level (easy reading)   = grade 1

Instructional reading level (needs teacher assistance) = grade 2

Frustration reading level (too difficult to make sense) = grade 3

Although he reads fairly fluently, rarely miscuing, Gill demonstrates minimal understanding of what he has read, missing details and main-idea questions. When he begins reading, he seldom predicts what might happen, and when he does, the predictions are random, usually based on a single detail.

Gill seems to enjoy journal writing and readily participates in this activity. He is often anxious to share what he has written and has selected some journal pieces for revision and editing during writing workshop time. For the most part, he demonstrates adequate use of sound-symbol relationships. Although fairly fluent in his writing, he tends to leave out important details, demonstrating a relatively poor sense of audience at this point in the school year (fall term).

Questions

What did you discover as you reviewed Gill's literacy behaviors? In the space provided beneath each phase of the diagnostic process, write down your notes.

Reflection

◆

◆

◆

Observation

◆

◆

◆

Translation

◆

◆

◆

Analysis

◆

◆

◆

Interpretation

◆

◆

◆

FOLLOW-UP DISCUSSION

In this activity you had an opportunity to experience the mental activity of theorizing that the diagnostic process requires. You began by *observing* Gill's reading and writing behaviors through accounts of his ability and performance and through samples of his writing. In particular, you examined some characteristics of Gill's writing as demonstrated in his journal. You perhaps noticed that he wrote a fine defense in the Nike vs. Reebok issue! In your noticing, you were *analyzing* his writing behaviors: his sense of audience, word choice, understanding of mechanics, and writing fluency.

Following your analysis of the writing samples in conjunction with other data in the case study, you probably decided that Gill has some definite strengths, such as his understanding and use of the graphophonemic system. Your knowledge of literacy development may have also suggested that he is a transitional speller who is capable of learning certain phonic rules and patterns, such as the silent *e* rule. You may have also determined that Gill demonstrates a good sense of story structure, which can be used to his advantage in story writing. Keeping in mind these strengths, you probably also realized he has some definite needs, especially in developing his ability to construct meaning as he reads print. As you synthesized the information about Gill, you were *interpreting* the data—making it meaningful by using your knowledge base.

Undoubtedly, your interpretations quickly gave way to translation as you began to consider the instructional techniques you might use if you were Gill's teacher. For example, you may have decided to capitalize on Gill's interest in sports to encourage his reading. Using Gill's strengths in free writing, you may have decided to have Gill write in his journal about the sports articles he read. This would use his strengths (decoding and sense of story in his writing) and preferences (free-choice activities and interest in sports) to develop reading comprehension. In making suggestions like this, you were *translating* the analysis and interpretation of your observations into instructional action.

Finally, in looking back over the notes you made about your observations, analysis, interpretation, and translation, you were reflecting on your own theorizing about Gill's literacy behaviors. In effect, you were distancing yourself from the situation, which allowed you to reconsider your decisions, assessing their appropriateness and consistency. By reflecting on various aspects of the process and thinking about how they fit together, you were able to construct a rationale for your judgments and your instruction, while simultaneously elaborating your personal beliefs. In sum, you used a diagnostic process to thoughtfully make instructional decisions which, in the end, is the important work of teaching.

Summary

The activities in this chapter provided you with opportunities to deepen your understanding of diagnosis as a process that is cognitively complex, dynamic, and ongoing. Beginning with the general problem solving we do every day, you were introduced to the mental activity of theorizing: asking yourself questions, risking guesses, making inferences, and drawing conclusions. These commonly used behaviors form the basis of the diagnostic process.

Next you were introduced to a model of the diagnostic process that can be used in the diagnostic teaching of reading. Each of its phases was described:

◆ Observation, which involves sensitive and informed looking using multiple indicators of performance
◆ Analysis, where attributes and patterns of an individual's reading behaviors are identified and compared to healthy reading processes
◆ Interpretation, which entails bringing meaning to the data using one's professional expertise, experience, and intuitions
◆ Translation, where instructional adjustments and techniques are suggested
◆ Reflection, which engages the teacher in rethinking the diagnosis, and constructing a rationale for decisions and instructional adjustments

Finally, you tried your hand at the process of diagnosis, examining the contents of an abbreviated case study. As a result, you experienced the theorizing that reading diagnosis requires and practiced the skills needed to assist problem readers.

Further Reading

Barr, R., Sadow, M., & Blachowicz, C. (1990). *Reading diagnosis for teachers* (2nd ed.). New York: Longman. Helps classroom teachers acquire the knowledge and skills necessary for classroom-based reading diagnosis and instructional planning.

Gipe, J. (1987). *Corrective reading techniques* (Chapter 2). Scottsdale, AZ: Gorsuch Scarisbrick. Describes the analytic process with respect to reading diagnosis and instructional intervention.

Holdaway, D. (1979). *The foundations of literacy.* Portsmouth, NH: Heinemann. Presents an inquiry about how children learn to read and write, and explores theoretically based solutions to the realities of practice.

Walker, B. (1992). *Diagnostic teaching of reading: Techniques for instruction and assessment* (2nd ed.). New York: Merrill/Macmillan. Chapter 3 describes the reflective process and Chapter 7 describes how to formulate diagnostic questions.

CHAPTER THREE

◆

The Tools and Procedures of Reading Diagnosis

◆

*To make wise application of our knowledge, its discriminate parts must
be integrated.*
—Henry Smith and Emerald Dechant

In the last chapter, we introduced you to a model of the diagnostic process, and you explored the mental activity of theorizing, which is central to diagnosis. In this chapter, we focus on more concrete and specific aspects of reading diagnosis, namely, the assessment tools and procedures that are used in the diagnostic process and in teaching.

Tools: Formal and informal assessments teachers use to obtain samples of individuals' reading behaviors.

Let's begin by looking at tools. Every profession has its **tools**—real objects used to get jobs done. Architects have mechanical rules; scientists have laboratory glassware; and doctors have surgical instruments. As teachers, we have assessments, or "tests," that help us sample learners' behaviors in some systematic way. However, as in all professions, the tool is only as good as the person using it. Assessment tools don't make diagnosis meaningful; teachers do.

In reading diagnosis, there are two main categories of assessment tools: formal and informal. **Formal assessment tools** sample reading behaviors in a controlled, prescribed fashion. How to administer, score, and interpret the assessment are carefully described, usually in a step-by-step manner. Using experimental procedures, the reliability (consistency), validity (authenticity), and norms (representativeness) of the assessment are determined previously. The *California Achievement Test* (1992), the *Gates-MacGinitie Reading Test* (1989), and the *Woodcock-Johnson Psychoeducational Battery* (1977) are some examples of formal assessment tools. Information pertinent to formal assessment will be discussed in greater depth in Chapter Nine.

Informal assessment tools are tests that have not been standardized; they do not use statistical procedures to determine norms, reliability, and validity. They vary widely in structure, format, and purpose, resembling instructional techniques more than "tests." Usually these assessment tools are used in natural classroom contexts because they do not require special conditions or physical arrangements. For instance, the Directed Reading-Thinking Activity (DR-TA), an instructional technique, can also be used as an informal assessment tool to observe children's predicting and confirming behaviors in a classroom reading situation. You will be introduced to a number of informal assessment tools of this type in the assessment tool catalog included in Activity 3.1.

Procedures: Guides teachers use to facilitate the analysis and summarization of information collected about an individual's reading behaviors.

Where assessment tools are used to gather information or data, **procedures** are used to guide teachers in using these tools and the information they yield. As in other professions, teachers of reading use specific procedures to facilitate their analysis and summarization of data. These procedures transform data into forms useful for instructional decision making and change, for example, miscue analysis

35

and retelling analysis. Knowing what procedures to use, and when, is crucial in the diagnostic process since these procedures assist the teacher in making sense of children's reading behaviors and foreshadow the instructional techniques that influence reading success.

The activities in this chapter are designed to acquaint you with several assessment tools, some of which double as instructional techniques easily applied in the classroom. You will also learn some basic analytical procedures that will facilitate the processing of observational information. In particular, you will

◆ examine a catalog of informal assessment tools and identify the basic purpose of each tool;

◆ create an Assessment Tool Quick Reference Card for your own use as a classroom teacher;

◆ read case studies of teachers, who are using assessment tools and analytical procedures, for the purpose of constructing your own Procedures Guide;

◆ practice using assessment tools and analytical procedures on your own.

As you work through the activities in this chapter, be mindful that they are introductory in nature, meant primarily to acquaint you with basic assessment tools and analytical procedures. Because of their scope, these are areas you will continually develop as a professional teacher, extending and enhancing your knowledge in both. To process the information assessment tools provide, we suggest that you seek concrete examples of as many assessment tools as possible, along with the procedures that regularly accompany these tools. Perhaps your instructor, a colleague, or a classroom teacher to whom you are assigned may assist you in this regard. We also urge you to practice using as many assessment tools and procedures as possible on your own.

ACTIVITY 3.1   Creating an Assessment Tool Quick Reference Card

(*Note:* Try this activity with a partner.)

What to Do First: Have you ever seen the *Whole Earth Catalog* (1971) or the *Whole Language Catalog* (Goodman, Bird, & Goodman, 1991)? Both of these publications provide a little information on a lot of related topics, serving as a collection of ideas about a major area.

Borrowing this format, we have gathered together a range of informal assessment tools into an Assessment Tool Catalog, providing a bit of information about each one. In our catalog, you will find some informal assessment tools that you may already know about, such as the informal reading inventory or a sight-word list. Others may be new to you, like the Print Orientation Assessment (Gillet & Temple, 1990) or the Metacomprehension Index (Schmitt, 1990).

To begin this activity, read through each item in the catalog. As you read about each tool, note the specific use of that tool. For example, some assessment tools are used to determine an individual's reading interests, others to find his reading level.

At the end of each item in the catalog, there is space to jot down a word or two that describes the tool's purpose. Do so for each item. Later, you will use these one- and two-word descriptors to construct your Assessment Tool Quick Reference Card. To help you get started with the catalog, the first item has been done for you. As we mentioned earlier, if possible, try to locate concrete examples of those tools you are completely unfamiliar with, so that you can further enhance your familiarity with that tool.

Assessments for Emerging and Beginning Readers

Print Orientation Assessment

(Gillet & Temple, 1990)
Modeled after Clay's Concepts About Print Test (1979), the Print Orientation Assessment measures young children's basic orientation to books and print. Specifically, it assesses left-to-right, top-to-bottom awareness; sense of word and letter; and the ability to distinguish between picture and print as story source. No special materials are required, only a storybook.

Descriptor:

Basic Print Concepts

Spelling Features

By asking the child to write down individual words, his or her spelling development stage may be determined.

Descriptor:

Running Record

Using an appropriate reading selection, a reader's cueing systems for print processing may be observed. Highly useful, this tool can easily be used in most classrooms.

Descriptor:

DL-TA

A variation of the familiar DR-TA, the Directed Listening-Thinking Activity can be used as a tool to assess children's abilities to predict, confirm, and integrate texts being read to them. It taps listening comprehension.

Descriptor:

Dictated Language Experience

Based on the Language-Experience Approach (LEA), this measure assesses oral language quality (fluency, use of descriptive words and complex sentences). It can also be used as a shared reading experience to note reading attempts.

Descriptor:

Speech-to-Print Match

(Gillet & Temple, 1990)
Using a familiar four-line poem, this assessment tool is used to observe sense of word and ability to learn new words. After the teacher reads a poem, the child reads it, demonstrating ability to match speech to print. Easy to administer, this tool yields substantial information.

Descriptor:

Sight-Word List

A graded list of words most frequently encountered in print, sometimes referred to as high-frequency words. There are many lists available, such as Dolch and Sakiey-Fry. Most reading programs have a list. Children are asked to read the list of words. The assessment goal is to determine to what extent a child can recognize the words rapidly through visual memory. Word-analysis strategies can also be examined.

Descriptor:

Cloze Assessment

Easy to administer to individuals or groups, this assessment simply involves deleting every seventh word from a passage. May be used to obtain reading level.

Descriptor:

Assessments for Developing Readers

Writing Samples

These include examples of an individual's writing efforts over time. Using holistic scoring, the samples can be analyzed for unity, organization, sense of audience, and mechanics. (*See also* Glazer & Searfoss, 1988.)

Descriptor:

Fluency Rating Scale

A 3-point rating scale for evaluating children's reading fluency; the scale uses the following levels:
◆ labored, disfluent
◆ slow and choppy
◆ good pace
A rating of 1 indicates disfluent reading, 2 a mild amount of stress, and 3 fluent, independent reading.

Descriptor:

The DR-TA

A familiar teaching strategy, the Directed Reading-Thinking Activity can also be used to assess individuals' abilities to predict, confirm, and integrate text meaning. Does require construction of a rating scale to evaluate the quality of an individual's predicting, confirming, and integrating skills.

Descriptor:

The Names Test

(Cunningham, 1990)
A test of decoding ability, this tool consists of 25 first and last names which individuals are asked to read. It provides a general impression of how a person decodes words using graphophonemic knowledge. Fun, fast, and easy to administer.

Descriptor:

The Informal Reading Inventory

Highly efficient, this tool consists of a series of graded passages that are read orally and silently. During oral reading, miscues are marked to assess print processing. During oral and silent reading, retellings are conducted to assess meaning processing. Questions are also asked, when necessary. Overall reading level may be determined based on oral and silent reading of passages. Used with children experiencing difficulty, the tool is most useful for assisting instructional decision making.

Descriptor:

The Metacomprehension Index

(Schmitt, 1990)
A questionnaire to measure the reader's awareness of comprehension strategies, this tool attempts to tap one's own thinking about comprehension. It can reveal what readers think they should do before, during, and after reading.

Descriptor:

Retelling

An alternative to comprehension questions after reading, readers are asked to "retell" what they have read. They are encouraged to relate the content as if the listener had not read the selection. Inferences about a reader's comprehension can be made based on the quality of the retelling. Rating scales are needed to assess quality.

Descriptor:

Spelling Features List

(Gillet & Temple, 1990)
This assessment provides insights about a learner's stage
of spelling development. Spelling attempts of words with
certain word features are scored holistically as prephonemic, early phonemic, letter-name, transitional, or correct.

Descriptor:

_____

Content Area Reading Inventory

(Vacca & Vacca, 1989)
Content Area Reading Inventory (CARI) is an informal,
teacher-made assessment that measures performance in
content-area reading matter. The focus is on *how* students read content. Kept simple, the tool provides information about comprehension, vocabulary skills, and
reading rate.

Descriptor:

_____

Content Area DR-TA

The same as the DR-TA strategy, only using informational
text. It indicates how a reader predicts, confirms, and integrates expository writing. Development of a rating scale
is necessary.

Descriptor:

_____

Assessments for Determining Readers' Attitudes, Interests, and Beliefs

Heathington Attitude Surveys

(Heathington, B., 1975)
Using common statements about reading, this tool measures an individual's attitude in six specific areas: free
reading, organized reading, at the library, at home, recreational reading, and general reading. Quick and reliable, it
is a boon to the classroom teacher.
Note: Primary and Intermediate Form

Descriptor:

_____

Elementary Reading Attitude Survey

(McKenna & Kear, 1990)
A quick indicator of student attitudes about reading, this
survey includes 20 items that explore attitudes toward
recreational and academic reading.

Descriptor:

_____

The Reading Interview

(Goodman & Burke, 1987)
By asking a person to respond to five general questions
about the reading process, perceptions and beliefs about
reading may be tapped. Simple to use and revealing,
there are many variations of this tool available which ap-
peal to different age levels.

Descriptor:

_____

Interest Inventory

This tool contains questions, sentence stems, and lists
that reveal specific reading interests, such as sports, biog-
raphy, and so on. Other interest areas may also be probed,
such as hobbies and TV watching.

Descriptor:

_____

What to Do Next: As we mentioned earlier, our catalog lists some basic informal assessment tools; you will learn about many others in your development as a teacher of reading. At this point, we will guide you in making a Quick Reference Card that includes the tools listed in our catalog. As you learn about other tools in future courses and workshops, you can add them to the card.

Look at the chart format on the next page. When completed, this will be your Assessment Tool Quick Reference Card. To construct it, do the following:

- ◆ First, in the column marked *Assessment Tools,* make a list of all the assessment tools found in the catalog. You may choose to add other assessments discussed in other courses or that you have used in your field work.
- ◆ Next, in the spaces running across the top of the chart (marked *Features*), list all of the descriptors you wrote in the catalog. Of course, you may add more descriptors if you choose to do so.
- ◆ Finally, fill in the chart by reading the name of the first assessment tool on your list. Then read across the Features row. Make a + mark in the box if the tool possesses that feature or characteristic. Make a − mark if it does not.

When finished, you will have constructed a Quick Reference Card for your use as a classroom teacher. This reference card is actually a features matrix or grid that provides a systematic way for organizing information about any topic. You may want to consider using this format in other ways in your own teaching. For now, on one card you have organized basic information about several assessment tools and what they do, so that you have a quick reference when you need it in your instructional work.

Assessment Tool Quick Reference Card

Features

Assessment Tools

FOLLOW-UP DISCUSSION

You probably have heard the following comment in some form or another: To do the job you have to have the right tool. Our catalog only provides a sampling of the informal assessment tools available to you as a teacher. Others may be found in the textbooks used in your reading courses, may be recommended in classroom materials, or may be suggested by classroom teachers with whom you work.

This is not to say that you will use all of these tools all of the time. You do, however, need to be familiar with many of them. Different instructional situations require different tools; in your educational work, you must decide which tool to use, when, and why. For example, a first grader may be struggling with beginning reading activities. In this instance, an assessment of the child's basic concepts about print would provide important insights for planning instruction. A thirteen-year-old's similar struggles, however, may be rooted in misperceptions about how reading works, which may become clarified best through a reading perceptions interview.

Thus, as we have expressed in previous chapters, it is the teacher who must make choices. Clearly the more informed those choices are, the more likely they will support children's reading development and growth. Selecting appropriate informal assessment tools, then, is another example of the teacher's responsibility to be knowledgeable so as to make well-grounded diagnostic decisions.

Now that you are familiar with some of the informal tools that can be used to diagnose reading behaviors, you need to know how to use them and how to process the information they provide. In short, you need to become familiar with the procedures that accompany the use of different assessment tools. This is the primary objective of the next activity. In it you will read nine case studies of teachers who are selecting assessment tools and then using diagnostic procedures to understand the reading behaviors of individuals. As a result of your reading, you will construct a Procedures Guide for your own use in diagnostic teaching.

Throughout your examination of these case studies, we encourage you to remain alert to two important ideas:

Assessment tools and procedures facilitate the observation, analysis, and interpretation of reader behaviors.

1. We use assessment tools and procedures to help us analyze or "take apart" a person's reading behaviors. Our aim is threefold: (1) to identify attributes or characteristics of an individual's reading behavior, (2) to identify relationships and patterns with respect to that behavior; and (3) to compare these with healthy literacy processes. As insightful as our analytic findings may be, however, they are only useful if thoughtfully applied to reading instruction that enhances the development of the whole person.

The fundamental goal of reading is the construction of meaning with written language.

2. Readers process print and meaning. Print processing is the reader's attempt to process the surface structure of a text or the printed symbols as they appear. This is largely a matter of using one's language systems in a productive way, that is, the syntactic, graphophonemic, semantic, and pragmatic systems. Meaning processing is the reader's effort to process the deep structure of the text. This has to do primarily with the construction of meaning or comprehension of the author's message. Through our assessment tools and analytical procedures, we may look more so at one of these processes than the other for the purpose of targeting our instruction. However, it should be kept in mind that print and meaning processing are co-occurring and interdependent, each influencing and informing the other. In the end, reading is preeminently a meaning-making endeavor.

ACTIVITY 3.2   **Constructing a Procedures Guide**

(*Note:* Try this activity on your own.)

What to Do: This activity is extensive and will require considerable time, so you may wish to spread it across several days. In brief, you will study nine cases of teachers using assessment tools and analytic procedures. Based on the descriptions of their work, you will construct a Procedures Guide, which describes what to do with specific assessment tools and why. Close study of these cases lays the groundwork for your own diagnosis of real readers and writers.

Carefully read each case study, locating the assessment tool in your catalog. Having familiarized yourself with the case and the tool being used, turn to the Procedure Section that follows each case study. At the top of the section, write the name and descriptor of the assessment tool. Then complete the procedure list and the analysis frame by filling in the blank spaces. Use the case study and your own previous learning experiences as sources of information.

Finally, compile the cases into a Procedures Guide, which you then can use as a reference. We are confident that you will find it quite helpful in your classroom work.

Case Study A: Assessing Instructional Reading Level

Miscue: An oral reading error.

Margi had just met Angie, a third grader who, according to her parents, has a history of reading difficulty. However, Margi had no other information about Angie. At their first meeting, Margi asked Angie to read a short sample from a third-grade text. First, Angie read aloud two paragraphs from a story so Margi could sample her oral reading. When Angie miscued or deviated from the text, Margi marked the deviations above the words as they were miscalled. In this way, she made a record of how Angie read the paragraphs. When Angie stopped reading for more than 5 seconds, Margi assisted her by supplying the word that was causing difficulty. She placed the letter *p* over the word that she supplied. Margi circled the words that Angie omitted, and put a caret and added those words that Angie inserted. After Angie read a paragraph, Margi asked Angie questions about the paragraph to see if she understood what she read. Specifically, she asked about the character and his problem, some key events, and the meaning of an important vocabulary word. At the same sitting, Margi asked Angie to silently read the next two paragraphs. After Angie was finished reading, Margi asked questions similar to those she asked before.

Scoreable miscue: An oral reading error that significantly disrupts the author's intended meaning.

Then Margi analyzed the performance on the oral reading and the silent reading selections. To do this, she counted the miscues on the oral paragraphs and divided the number of scoreable miscues into the number of words that Angie read, using the Error Rate Chart shown in Figure 3.1. This gave her an "error rate."

Then, Margi computed the percent of comprehension questions answered correctly. She compared these scores (error rate and comprehension percentage) with standards for quantitative reading performance, using the Scoring Criteria Chart in Figure 3.2. She observed if the paragraph was *just right* for instruction (instructional level), or if the paragraph was so *familiar* that it didn't need instruction (independent level), or if the paragraph was *too difficult* for Angie (frustration level).

Margi also sampled silent reading performance. She looked at the silent reading in the same fashion as oral reading. She computed the percent of comprehension questions answered correctly, then she compared this score with the standards for quantitative reading performance to see if the paragraph was just right for instruction and so on, again using the Scoring Criteria Chart in Figure 3.2.

When Margi looked at this assembled information, she realized that during both oral and silent reading, Angie had read with great difficulty. Therefore, Margi selected a story from a second-grade reading series to continue her evaluation. These paragraphs were also read at instructional level. Margi then found an easier text to try to establish an independent level for Angie; however, Angie did not read any text at independent level. All the selections fell within the instructional range.

FIGURE 3.1
Error rate chart

1. Determine the number of scoreable errors per passage read.

   Example: Angie made 4 scoreable errors.

2. Estimate the total number of words in the passage read.

   Example: Angie read 86 words.

3. Divide the total number of words by the number of scoreable errors. Round off the quotient to the nearest whole number.

   Example: $\dfrac{21 \text{ r } 2}{4)\,86} = 21$

4. The quotient determined in Step 3 becomes the denominator in the error rate and the number 1 becomes the numerator.

   Example: Angie read the passage with 1 error every 21 running words; the error rate is 1/21.

Note. Reprinted with the permission of Macmillan Publishing Company from *Diagnostic Teaching of Reading: Techniques for Instruction and Assessment,* Second Edition by Barbara J. Walker. Copyright © 1992 by Macmillan Publishing Company.

FIGURE 3.2
Scoring criteria chart

Reading Level	Word Recognition Error Rate	Comprehension Percentage
Independent		
1–2	1/17+	80+
3–5	1/27+	85+
6+	1/35+	90+
Instructional		
1–2	1/8–1/16	55–80
3–5	1/13–1/26	60–84
6+	1/18–1/35	65–90
Frustration		
1–2	1/7–	55–
3–5	1/12–	60–
6+	1/17–	65–

Note: From *The Finger Count System for Monitoring Reading Behavior* (pp. 7–11) by W. R. Powell, 1981, unpublished paper. Adapted by permission of the author.

Assessment Tool: *Descriptor:*

Procedures

1. Select a passage and write _____ for two sections.

2. Have Angie _____ one section orally.

3. Mark _____ as Angie reads orally, then ask _____ .

4. Compute the error rate score and the _____ percentage score. Compare it to _____

    for quantitative reading performance to decide the _____ .

5. Repeat the sequence for _____ reading.

6. If the selections are in the _____ or _____ range, move to a more

    difficult text.

7. If the selections represent _____ level reading, move to an easier text.

8. Continue until the assessment includes a frustration level reading. The text just prior to frustration level is consid-

    ered the highest _____ level.

Analysis

Compare _____ and silent reading to standards for reading performance and decide if the passages are within

the _____ , _____ , or _____

range. Think about the performance on these tasks: Did the student exhibit more elaborate comprehension when

reading orally or silently? Did the miscues the student made affect comprehension?

Synopsis

This assessment tool helps teachers decide on an instructional level—a level where the student can profit from classroom instruction. It also helps the teacher identify whether the student has strengths in either oral or silent reading, or both. If the student has a strength in oral reading, then she has what is called **print processing strengths.** If the student has strengths in silent reading rather than oral reading (i.e., better silent comprehension than oral reading performance), then she has what is called **meaning processing strengths.** (The Running Record in the following section is another form of this assessment tool.)

Running Records

Running records (Clay, 1985) are powerful tools for assessing progress and the match between reader and text. When used as an informal tool, the student is asked to read a selection (about 50–100 words) aloud. The teacher counts the number of words that are miscued. For a story suitable for instruction, the student should not miss more than one word in ten. If the error rate is greater than this, another story should be chosen that is less challenging.

To elaborate this simple system, teachers can record the exact miscue and then compare it to the original text. This comparison can give insight into the cueing system the student is using (semantic, syntactic, graphophonemic). Teachers also can use the following form containing questions to evaluate miscues:

	Yes	Partially	No
1. Does the word make sense?			
2. Does the word fit grammatically in the sentence?			
3. Does the replacement word start with the same letter(s)?			
4. Does the replacement word sound the same?			
5. Does the reader try to "sound out" the word?			

The teacher looks for a pattern of miscues over time. Evaluating the cueing systems helps the teacher match his instruction to what the student does.

Case Study B:
Assessing Angie's Knowledge of the Graphophonemic System

To evaluate Angie's knowledge of the graphophonemic system, Margi had Angie write a summary of the story she read in the second-level text. Margi took the writing and compared each word to a spelling assessment guide (Figure 3.3) to evaluate Angie's use of the graphophonemic system.

Margi made a list of the words used in the summary, correctly spelled, as well as how Angie spelled each word. Then she compared Angie's spellings with the spelling assessment guide. When Angie's spelling fit most of the descriptors in a category, Margi gave the word that rating.

Using the spelling assessment guide, Margi scored each word in the summary and added the scores together. Then Margi found the average level of spelling (graphophonemic) awareness by dividing the total score by the total number of words in the summary. Angie's pattern indicated that most of the time she was in the letter-naming stage—she assigned letters based on sounds as she heard them, using invented spelling but representing every sound heard. She did put spaces between words and had mastered letter formation.

Margi then compared these results to Angie's performance on the informal reading inventory. Both assessments indicated Angie's strategies were similar to other second-grade readers. Therefore, Margi concluded that Angie's knowledge of the graphophonemic system was developmentally appropriate and that she applied this knowledge when she read.

FIGURE 3.3
Spelling assessment guide

Spelling Features Assessment Guide

The following is a scale for assessing graphophonemic knowledge in a written sample. These ratings estimate children's spelling development and provide an average score of code knowledge.

Select a writing sample and score each word according to the guide. Characteristics of each spelling stage are provided.

Stage	*Characteristics*
Prephonemic (Score 0 for each word in this category.)	Letter forms designate a message No apparent graphophonemic relationships exhibited Writes and repeats known letters fairly well
Early phonemic (Score 1 for each word in this category.)	Whole word designated by 1 or more letters Letter designates some phonemes in the word Letter-naming haphazard and sparse
Letter-name (Score 2 for each word in this category.)	Writes a letter for more than half the phonemes in the word Designates phonemes with a letter name Uses spaces between words
Transitional (Score 3 for each word in this category.)	Graphophonemic relationships based on conventional spelling Conventional rules used suitably, but not accurately (e.g., "battel" for "battle") Transposes some letters in words
Conventional (Score 4 for each word in this category.)	Uses standard spellings Whole word spelled accurately

Total Score _____

Average Score = total score ÷ total number of words in sample

Assessment Tool: *Descriptor:*

Procedures

1. Have the student _____ either her own story or a _____ of a story she has read.

2. Make a list of how the words would be spelled _____ and how the student

    _____ each word.

3. Score each _____ using the _____ assessment guide.

4. Add the score for each word to get a total score and divide by the _____ number of words in the selection.

5. Using the descriptors in the guide, describe the student's strategies.

Analysis

The _____ assessment score gives you an idea of the learner's _____

knowledge or how he uses letters and _____ together.

Synopsis

This assessment helps to evaluate a student's knowledge and use of the graphophonemic system. When compared to the student's performance on the informal reading inventory, decisions about the student's print processing can be made.

Case Study C:
Assessing Angie's Retelling of a Story

Margi asked Angie to read the first chapter in *Frog and Toad Together* (Lobel, 1972) and retell the story as if she were telling it to a friend who had never heard it. Margi audiotaped the retelling so she could refer to it later when she scored the retelling.

After Angie retold the story, Margi used the retelling score guide in Figure 3.4 to assess how elaborate the retelling was.

She evaluated whether Angie began with an introduction, and indeed, Angie used an introduction. Next, she assessed whether Angie discussed the main character along with other characters. Angie had a good understanding of the main character, but did not mention any other characters. She definitely understood the main problem, relating it to her own recent birthday. As she retold the action, Angie mixed up the order and constantly said, "Well, I forgot the rest." However, she retold most of the key plot episodes. Angie did forget to explain the resolution and end her retelling. Since Angie retold less than 70 percent of the story, Margi assessed that understanding how stories are formed, a meaning processing task, was definitely an area of concern for Angie.

Assessment Tool: *Descriptor:*

Procedures

1. Have the student read a story that is not too _____ .

2. Then ask the student to _____ the story as if he/she were telling it to a _____ .

3. Tape record the retelling.

4. Use the _____ guide to evaluate the retelling.

5. Evaluate whether the retelling contained an _____ and main

   _____ .

6. Evaluate whether the student stated the _____ character's problem and goal.

7. Evaluate whether the student stated the important _____ of the story.

8. Evaluate how the student ended the story and if he/she stated the _____ .

Analysis

One indication of _____ is knowledge of story structure. In this assessment, the student needs to remember at least _____ to 80 percent of the story. The teacher further analyzes what particular parts of the story (setting, _____ events, resolution) the student _____ and what parts he or she needs assistance with.

Synopsis

As an assessment tool, a retelling evaluates a student's knowledge and use of story structure, or how stories are formed, as an aid to comprehension. The quality of the student's retelling can be compared to how well the student answered comprehension questions. Moreover, the extent to which questions enhanced the student's ability to process meaning can be examined. Thus, retelling assessment, which employs retelling analysis and questioning strategies, gives the teacher further knowledge about a student's meaning processing with print.

FIGURE 3.4
Retelling score guide

Retelling Assessment of a Story

The following guide provides a quantitative score for a retelling of a story. Sometimes a teacher might have to give prompts during the retelling, but the idea is to evaluate each student's ability to retell the story without teacher assistance.

Scoring Guide for a Retelling Assessment of a Story

Setting

4   Contains an introduction, names of important characters, and elaboration of significant places and times

3   Contains principal character and other characters; short explanation of place and time

2   Contains principal character and mentions times or places

1   Contains only one component, such as place, or names of insignificant characters

0   Does not contain any factors pertaining to setting

Rating (0–4) _____

Problem

4   Contains an explanation of the principal character's major goal or problem to be solved, including theme of the story; also includes the incident that sets up the problem in the story

3   Contains major problem the principal character needs to resolve

2   Contains only a vague explanation of the problem

1   Contains an irrelevant problem

0   Does not describe any conflict

Rating (0–4) _____

Events

4   Contains important events or plot episodes that lead to resolution. Most events or episodes recounted are related to attempts to work out the problem, are a result of this action, or are the character's response to the episode

3   Contains important events and some of these involve attempts to work out the problem, a result of this action, or the character's response to the episode

2   Contains some important events but does not embellish them

1   Contains only a few irrelevant events

0   Does not contain any important events

Rating (0–4) _____

Resolution

4   Concludes retelling so there is a sense of progression and recounts how the problem was resolved and the goal reached

3   Concludes retelling so there is a sense of progression and vaguely relates how the problem was resolved

2   Concludes retelling so there is a sense of progression, but does not relate how the problem was resolved

1   Concludes retelling abruptly

0   Ends retelling halfway through the story

Rating (0–4) _____
TOTAL SCORE _____

Case Study D:
Assessing Mark's Ability to Match Speech to Print

Vance, a first-grade teacher, needed more information on Mark, a new student in his class. Mark seemed inattentive in class and Vance wanted to know about his emerging literacy. First, Vance read a predictable book, *I Love Ladybugs* by Roach Van Allen (1985), aloud to Mark.

After asking Mark a few questions about the story, Vance read the first two lines of the book again, and asked Mark to repeat those lines, pointing to the words in the text as Mark said them. On a separate sheet of paper, Vance noted the similarity between what Mark said and what the text contained. He made a check mark for every word that Mark repeated and a minus for those he did not repeat.

Since the first pages of this particular book are extremely easy, Vance then read two lines in the middle of the book where the language structure is more difficult. Again he made a check mark for every word that Mark pointed to and repeated and a minus for each he did not.

In both instances, Mark was able to point to and repeat the words as if he were matching each word he said to the words in the text. Thus, Vance looked for a more complicated assessment task, concluding that Mark could match speech to print easily.

Assessment Tool: *Descriptor:*

Procedures

1. Read a _____ book or poem aloud to the student.

2. Next discuss the _____ .

3. Read a few _____ from the story.

4. Ask the student to _____ and _____ to those same lines.

5. As the student reads, make a _____ for every word read correctly and a

   _____ for those read incorrectly.

Analysis

This assessment gives you an idea of the student's _____ of a word and whether or not he/she

can match oral _____ to words and sentences found in _____ .

Synopsis

This assessment tool helps to evaluate the student's developing knowledge of printed language. By matching what he/she hears to the words on the page, the reader illustrates that he/she understands the function of print and that print carries meaning.

Case Study E:
Assessing Mark's Concepts about Print

Vance wanted to know more about Mark's literacy development, so he had Mark answer a few questions about a predictable book. He handed the book to Mark and asked him to open it. When Mark did this, Vance noticed how he handled the book and whether or not Mark knew how to position the book to open it. To see if Mark knew where the print was on the page, Vance asked Mark where he should begin reading. Then Vance asked Mark where to read next. Mark quickly showed Vance how to turn the page and begin reading on the left-hand page and then on the right-hand page. This showed Vance that Mark knew how readers move from the top to the bottom of the page, and that they begin at the left of a line and go along the line to the right, then return to the next line on the left margin.

Next Vance gave Mark two index cards and asked him to frame one word, two words, one letter, and two letters. Vance learned that Mark knew the concept of a word because he was able to find the beginning of a word. Mark was uncertain about the concept of a letter, however, which he demonstrated by moving the card to random places to indicate a letter.

Vance then read a line of the story and asked Mark to repeat it. Mark read the line exactly as Vance read it, not reading too many or too few words. Following this, Vance read an entire page and asked Mark to read it twice. As Mark reread the story, he said the same thing as Vance, which indicated to Vance that Mark knew words remained the same each time you read them.

Vance asked Mark to name a letter in a word on the page they were reading. Mark was uncertain, guessing randomly from the letter names he knew. Vance asked him to write his name and name the letters. Mark readily wrote his name and named the letters, which indicated that Mark understood that the same word always has the same spelling. But, Mark did not know the names of letters in unfamiliar words.

Based on this assessment, Vance concluded that Mark possessed many basic concepts about print, including (1) how to hold a book, (2) where the print begins and ends, (3) reading occurs from left to right, (4) concept of word and letter, (5) speech-to-print match, and (6) consistency of print. He did not, however, have a well-developed knowledge of letter names. Figure 3.5 shows a sample of the assessment guide that Vance used.

FIGURE 3.5
Concepts about print guide

Concepts about Print

The following is an adaptation of Marie Clay's *Concepts about Print Test* (Clay, 1985). These procedures can be used with any piece of children's literature.

Concepts about Print Interview

1. Hand the student a book and ask the student to open it. Does the child know that the spine goes on the left?
   Notes:

2. Ask the student to show you where you should begin reading. Does the student know the story begins where the print begins?
    Notes:

3. Ask where you should go next. Does the student know that the left-hand page comes before the right-hand page? That you move from the top to the bottom of the page? That you begin at the left and go along the line to the right and that you return to the next line on the left margin?
    Notes:

4. Give the student two index cards and ask him to frame one word, two words, one letter, and two letters. Does the student know the concepts of word and letter?
    Notes:

5. Read a line of the story and ask the student to repeat it. Does the student know when he read too many or too few words?
    Notes:

6. Read an entire page and ask the student to read it twice after you do. As the student rereads stories, does he say the same thing? Does the child realize that texts remain the same?
    Notes:

7. Ask the student to name a letter in any word on the page, then ask him to write his name and name the letters. Does the student understand that the same word always has the same spelling?
    Notes:

Assessment Tool: *Descriptor:*

Procedures

1. _____ a book to a student, and notice how he/she handles it.

2. Ask the student where to _____ reading and where to read _____ .

3. Give the student two _____ and ask him/her to frame a _____ . Then ask him/her to frame a _____ .

4. Read a _____ of the story and have the student _____ it.

5. Ask the student to _____ a letter in a word.

6. Ask the student to write his/her _____ and _____ the letters.

Analysis

Through this procedure you analyze what the student understands about _____ print works. Also the traditional skill of knowledge of _____ names is evaluated in the context of a real story.

Synopsis

This assessment tool allows the teacher to identify the student's basic concepts about print, indicating the student's emerging knowledge about how to process print.

Case Study F:
Assessing Geraldo's Meaning Construction

Carol is teaching a lesson in third grade and is curious about Geraldo's reading behavior. As she teaches the story *Sam, Bangs and Moonshine* (Ness, 1966), she watches Geraldo in the group setting. Sometimes she asks him questions directly, but mostly she watches how he responds during the lesson.

First, she reads the title and asks the students to predict what might happen in the story. They read a few pages, and then Carol asks Geraldo what happened. Then she asks him if what happened is what he had predicted, and if he, as well as the others, want to keep their predictions.

They read to another stopping point and she repeats her line of questioning. This time she asks Geraldo to explain why he thinks Sam will get punished. Finally, they finish the story and Carol asks Geraldo to summarize the story.

DR-TA: The directed reading-thinking activity—a reader strategy that encourages the reader, while reading, to predict, confirm, and integrate with respect to the author's message.

Then Carol takes out a rating scale for evaluating responses from a DR-TA and evaluates Geraldo's predictions, source of information, and summarization as illustrated in Figure 3.6.

Using this assessment, Carol lists the strategies that Geraldo is using as he constructs meaning, as well as how close his interpretations match those of the author's.

FIGURE 3.6
DR-TA evaluation rating guide

DR-TA Evaluation

	Yes 3	*Somewhat* 2	*No* 1

Predicts

Makes predictions easily	|------------------------------------|		
Uses prior experiences	|------------------------------------|		
Uses title or pictures	|------------------------------------|		
Uses textual information	|------------------------------------|		

Confirms and monitors

Checks predictions	|------------------------------------|		
Revises predictions as needed	|------------------------------------|		
Justifies responses	|------------------------------------|		
Uses prior experiences	|------------------------------------|		
Uses text examples	|------------------------------------|		
Rereads when necessary	|------------------------------------|		

Integrates

Elaborates responses	|------------------------------------|		
Applies prior experiences	|------------------------------------|		
Applies text examples	|------------------------------------|		
Connects text and personal experiences	|------------------------------------|		
Compares stories to other stories	|------------------------------------|		

Summarizes

Includes important information	|------------------------------------|		
Makes critical inferences	|------------------------------------|		
Provides well-formed responses	|------------------------------------|		

Geraldo predicts using the text, but fails to use his background knowledge to elaborate either his predictions or his summaries. In fact, his summaries are quite sparse, highlighting only specific facts found in the text. He does not appear to reorganize the information by using both what he knows and important textual information.

Assessment Tool: *Descriptor:*

Procedures

1. Choose a story to read and ask the student to _____ what it might be about.

2. Read the story to a selected _____ point.

3. After the first section, ask the student to retell what is _____ .

4. Then ask if his/her _____ were on the right track and _____ he/she thinks that.

5. Continue with the sequence of making _____ , checking

   _____ , and _____ your response.

6. Evaluate the student's performance using a rating scale for a DR-TA.

Analysis

The information on the rating scale gives you information about how readily the student _____

what might possibly happen in the story, as well as what sources of information—the _____ or background

knowledge—the student is using. Finally, the scale can also provide information about how the student elaborates and

organizes a _____ of what has been read.

Synopsis

This assessment tool can be used as you are teaching a DR-TA (Directed Reading-Thinking Activity) lesson in the classroom setting. Simply watch closely a student as you ask him/her to predict and justify responses and to summarize his/her meaning processing. This information gives you an idea about how the student reconstructs the meaning of a story. You obtain information about the student's willingness to predict (or maintain an active stance), the source of information the student is using, as well as how elaborate his/her summarization can be.

Case Study G:
Assessing Geraldo's Reading Fluency

After Geraldo read the story, Carol wanted to check his fluency, so she asked Geraldo to read aloud his favorite part of the story. Geraldo read the section about when the storm came. Most of the time he was reading fluently, but when he came to the word *murky,* he stumbled and began to read word for word. Using the fluency rating scale in Figure 3.7, Carol rated his fluency as a three, which indicated he read the passage with some degree of fluency; however, much of his reading was in a monotone and he seldom stopped for punctuation marks.

FIGURE 3.7   **Fluency Assessment**
Fluency rating scale
_____

This measure indicates whether a student is automatically connecting what words look like with what they mean within a passage. This method has been validated and is simple to use (Zutell, 1988). The teacher asks a student to read a paragraph aloud, and then rates the paragraph by using the three-point scale that follows. A fluent reader would receive a score of 3, while a developing reader would score a 2. A score of 1 indicates that a reader is experiencing a great deal of stress and needs more opportunities to read easy selections and hear the teacher's model. Use the following three-point scale in rating the reader's oral fluency on a specific selection (Walker, 1992b).

Fluency Scale

◆ Nonfluent and hesitant reading, marked by delayed word-by-word reading, many pauses and repetitions where words are slowly sounded out, and/or a lack of intonation and expression (score 1 point)

◆ Reading is partially fluent and exhibits one of two processes: (1) sporadic and slow reading in two- and three-word phrases with pauses for sounding out or repeating words; (2) adequate pace marked by inconsistent phrasing and intonation patterns (score 2 points)

◆ Smooth and fluent reading, marked by a vigorous pace with longer phrases and appropriate use of expression and intonation (score 3 points)
_____

Assessment Tool: *Descriptor:*

Procedures

1. Have the student read _____ a section of a story.

2. Listen closely to how the student is _____ .

3. Notice the pauses, repetitions, and _____-out behaviors.

4. Notice if the reading is _____-by-word.

5. Notice the intonation.

6. Give the oral reading an overall rating using the _____ _____ scale.

Analysis

One indication of automatic _____ processing is how _____ the student can read. In this

assessment, the student must predict what the words are, using both his knowledge of word _____

and his own prior knowledge.

Synopsis

Fluent reading results from reading in phrases with a good sense of rhythm. There are only a few repetitions, and these
are to correct phrasing errors rather than word-recognition errors. This fluent reading indicates the reader is connecting
what words look like with their meaning and their use in sentences. The reader automatically predicts what the print
will say and checks both his/her own knowledge as well as the words on the page. This process involves the integration of print and meaning processing.

Case Study H:
Assessing Geraldo's Learning Log

Carol also wanted to gain additional insights about Geraldo's reading and writing behaviors. She had Geraldo keep a log about what he was reading in history. Each day, he was to reflect about what he was reading. Carol wrote a response once a week to what Geraldo had written in his log. After four weeks, she evaluated Geraldo's writing using a rubric for journal writing, as depicted in Figure 3.8.

Geraldo's responses contained single ideas; he seldom related larger concepts that tied events together. His responses were sparse, and even Carol's comments had not helped Geraldo elaborate his ideas. Geraldo's responses were very factual; he did not see the cause-effect nature of major historical events.

FIGURE 3.8
Journal/log assessment rating scale

Journal/Log Assessment Rating Scale

	Yes 4	Some 3	Little 2	No 1
Responses				
include details				
include main ideas				
acknowledge T comments				
increase in volume over time				
reflect current topics of study				
include emotional reactions				
indicate metacomprehension				
develop a concept/idea				

Assessment Tool: _____ *Descriptor:* _____

Procedures

1. Have the student read a story, trade book, or _____ book.

2. Each day have the student _____ in a learning log about what he/she is thinking about the reading.

3. At least once a week, _____ a response to log entries.

4. Periodically, evaluate the log entries using a _____ .

5. Notice the length, content, and type of information in the responses.

6. Write a description of the student's reading and writing behaviors.

Analysis

One indication of comprehension is what a student selects to include in a _____ entry. By evaluating the writing, the teacher has an idea of _____ information the student selected as important, how _____ the student's concepts and content knowledge are, and the extensiveness of the _____ response.

Synopsis

This assessment tool helps the teacher observe how a student uses writing to express his/her thinking and reading. By asking a student to write about what he/she reads, the teacher can evaluate the sources and type of information the student selects to construct meaning. The writing also can indicate how elaborate the student's thinking is, as well as his/her prior experience related to the topic.

Case Study I:
Assessing Penni's Perceptions about Reading

Steve was concerned about Penni's attitude toward reading. He felt that her attitude was affected by what she thought reading was. Therefore, he asked Penni questions about the reading process and researched her perceptions about reading by using the interview questions in Figure 3.9.

He asked Penni what she thought reading was. Penni answered that reading was getting all the words pronounced correctly. She did not realize that reading was a process of constructing meaning. Steve asked Penni who a good reader was in her class and why she thought that. Again, her response indicated her belief that good readers never have to repeat words and they automatically know meaning by pronouncing words. She had no idea how to help a friend who was having difficulty with reading. She simply answered, "I don't know." Likewise, the only strategy she had for recovering from difficulties when reading was to sound out words. Steve concluded that Penni was an extremely passive reader who had no notion of the strategies used in active reading.

Assessment Tool: *Descriptor:*

Procedures

1. Ask the student questions about what _____ is and what good _____ do.

2. Write the student's _____ on a sheet of paper.

3. Look for patterns to evaluate the student's _____ about the reading process.

Analysis

By conducting an _____ about the strategies of reading and what problems can arise,

the teacher finds out about the student's _____ of reading. This often indicates the

_____ that the student is using when reading becomes difficult.

Synopsis

This assessment tool evaluates students' perceptions about the nature of the reading process. Such information gives you an idea about the strategies students use when problems occur, as well as how they think about themselves as readers.

FIGURE 3.9
Reading interview
questions

The Reading Interview

Using a reading interview, this assessment taps beliefs about literacy (Goodman & Burke, 1987; Harlin, Lipa, & Lonberger, 1991). Some of the questions may include:

1. What is reading?
2. What is writing?
3. Who is a good reader that you know? What makes him or her a good reader?
4. Do you think you are a good reader? Why?
5. If some friends were having trouble reading, how could you help them?
6. When you are reading and come to something you don't know, what do you do?

**FOLLOW-UP
DISCUSSION**

Procedures are an important part of reading diagnosis. They provide ways for getting to know a problem or situation—for getting "inside" of it, noting parts and patterns. In other words, procedures help us to look at information in a systematic way and to organize the time we spend analyzing that information.

Realizing the importance of both systematic observation and time in classroom life, the more fluent you are with diagnostic procedures, the more quickly and effectively you can apply them to children's demonstrations of reading behavior in the course of classroom reading instruction. Indeed, this is essential to our overall goal: the inclusion of diagnosis in instruction in a way that is ongoing and informing.

Consequently, just as we learn to read by reading and to write by writing, we learn to diagnose by diagnosing. Becoming familiar and comfortable with the diagnostic procedures discussed in this activity is important for the successful integration of diagnosis and instruction. Hence, for the final activity, you will be asked to try out some assessment tools with children and to practice basic procedures. We encourage you to keep a log of your practice runs with assessment tools and their related procedures. This provides concrete evidence of your intent to become adept at the practice of diagnosis.

ACTIVITY 3.3   Logging Practice with Tools and Procedures
(*Note:* Try this activity on your own.)

What to Do: In this activity, you are encouraged to practice using one or two assessment tools along with their related procedures. Your choice of tools may involve you in activities such as miscue analysis, retelling analysis, holistic scoring, and interpreting performance on interviews or in reader strategies (e.g., DR-TA).

Schedule time to practice using one or two assessment tools with a child of your choice. Keep a log of your attempts. Each entry should include the date, the child's name and age, the assessment tool used, the procedures you used during and following the assessment, and an evaluation of the experience. The following format may be helpful in organizing your entries. Good luck, and don't forget to thank the children for assisting you!

Practice Log Format

Child's Name: Age:

Date: Assessment Tool:

Procedures During Assessment:

Procedures Following Assessment (e.g., miscue analysis, retelling analysis, holistic scoring, interpretation, other):

Evaluation:

Summary

The activities in this chapter provided opportunities for you to deepen your understanding of the practices fundamental to diagnosis. These include informal assessment tools and specific procedures that allow for the systematic observation and analysis of reading behaviors.

First you developed an Assessment Tool Quick Reference Card for your personal use. Next, you studied cases that described how various tools are used and what their related analytic procedures are (e.g., a fluency rating). While doing so, you constructed a Procedures Guide for use with different assessment tools. Finally, you were encouraged to practice using tools and basic diagnostic procedures, recognizing that practice develops your skill in using these in teaching. Although demanding, all of these activities prepare you for the case analyses to come, and ultimately, your own educational work.

Further Reading

Cooter, R. (1990). *The teacher's guide to reading tests.* Scottsdale, AZ: Gorcsuch Scarisbrick. Supplies reading teachers with a useful desk reference of informal reading inventories, diagnostic reading tests, and group reading tests.

Eggleton, J. (1990). *Whole language evaluation—reading, writing and spelling.* Bothell, WA: The Wright Group. Describes an approach and tools for the informal assessment of primary-level readers and writers.

Glazer, S., & Searfoss, L. (1988). *Reading diagnosis and instruction: A C-A-L-M approach* (Chapters 9 & 10 & Appendix B). Englewood Cliffs, NJ: Prentice-Hall. Includes a wide array of informal assessment tools and procedures, as well as a guide to formal reading tests.

Glazer, S., Searfoss, L., & Gentile, L. (Eds.). (1988). *Reexamining reading diagnosis—new trends and procedures.* Newark, DE: International Reading Association. Provides a number of informal assessments that easily can be used in the classroom setting.

Goodman, K., Goodman, Y., & Hood, W. (1989). *The whole language evaluation book.* Portsmouth, NH: Heinemann. Presents a collection of articles that describe whole-language evaluation processes, techniques, and procedures.

Johnston, P. (1992). *Constructive evaluation of literate activity* (Part II). New York: Longman. Provides an excellent description of how to record oral reading and how to interpret oral reading behaviors.

Rhodes, L., & Dudley-Marling, C. (1988). *Readers and writers with a difference* (Chapter 3). Portsmouth, NH: Heinemann. Describes an observational approach to the assessment of reading and writing, including miscue analysis.

PART TWO

Teaching Techniques and Instruction

For all our discussion of the foundations, the process, and the procedures of diagnosis, these are not its important goals. Their effective use in instruction is! In the end, knowing about diagnosis must give way to using it in teaching-learning interactions. For example, one teacher asked a student to read a familiar book, *The Purple Cow* (Burgess, 1961). When the student stumbled and could not figure out the word *bluebird,* the teacher asked: "What is the animal on this page? What color is it?" With these prompts, the student easily identified the unknown word. By focusing the reader's attention on both the words and the pictures, the teacher assisted the student's reading of the story. The teacher also concluded that, for this reader, instruction needed to include familiar books where the pictures explicitly cued the text.

In this example, the teacher diagnoses, using his knowledge base to observe, analyze, and interpret the instructional interaction, then translates his insights into his teaching. Moreover, he continually examines his own instruction, reflecting on his actions. As a result of his "reflection-in-action," he judges the effect of his teaching behaviors on readers' behaviors and makes appropriate instructional adjustments.

This use of diagnosis in meaningful instruction requires the sound knowledge and use of instructional techniques. Developing your knowledge in this respect is the aim of the first two chapters in Part Two. Through the activities in each, you will become acquainted with teaching techniques and the reader strategies these techniques develop. After all, that is the point of diagnosis and teaching: assisting readers so that they know how to do what they must do to use written language in ways that are meaningful and satisfying to them.

Consequently, in Chapters Four and Five you will work through several teaching techniques that support and extend reader strategies. Just so that we are clear in our terminology, let us reiterate: Teachers teach using techniques; readers read using strategies.

Since there are many instructional techniques, we have selected only those viewed as mainstays of reading instruction. These techniques have been organized into two groups: those that develop print processing (deciphering the actual printed text) and those that develop meaning processing (making meaning with text). We will begin with teaching techniques associated with print processing and, as in earlier chapters, we will involve you in activities that assist your understanding and use of these techniques.

65

The third chapter in this section, Chapter Six, affords you an opportunity to apply your understanding of the fundamentals of diagnosis and accompanying instructional techniques to an instructional routine.

The chapters in Part Two, then, detail the fundamentals of diagnosis discussed in Part One and provide practice in their use. Such practice is very necessary if diagnosis is to become embedded in instruction in real teaching and learning contexts.

CHAPTER FOUR

◆

Teaching Techniques and Reader Strategies for Print Processing

──────────── ◆ ────────────

The second major category of problem-solving tasks that face the [individual] in learning to read is understanding the technical linguistic concepts needed for reasoning about the relationships between speech and writing.
—John Downing

──────────────────────

Take a moment to look again at the psycholinguistic model of the reading process introduced in Chapter One. Recall from our discussion that this model depicts reading as a problem-solving process where readers make predictions, confirm them using print cues and their own schemata, and integrate what they are reading into what they already know. The purpose of this entire endeavor is to make sense of the author's printed message in a satisfactory way.

According to the psycholinguistic model, then, readers use the printed words and the meanings they associate with them to actively construct meaning while reading. This is a dynamic interaction involving the processing of the surface display of the print while constructing meaning with respect to the author's message. We refer to the reader's active involvement with printed symbols as print processing, that is, how readers cognitively "process" print cues and individual word meanings to assist in their attempts to make sense of the author's message. In this chapter we are particularly interested in how readers use their print processing abilities to read fluently and to problem solve when they come to words they do not know.

> Print processing is how readers cognitively "process" print cues and individual word meanings to assist in their attempts to make sense of the author's message.

Specifically, print processing involves readers in using their language systems—their semantic, syntactic, and graphophonemic systems—to make predictions about the printed symbols presented. Print processing encompasses those areas traditionally known as sight-word recognition, word analysis and decoding, using context clues, and reading fluency. In short, print processing utilizes many of those skills associated with the demonstration of word knowledge, for example, recall of high-frequency words and understanding and using specific word features (distinctive visual features, prefixes, suffixes, vowel sounds, and so on).

More than merely possessing these skills, however, print processing is the reader's successful *orchestration* of them while reading. The successful coordination of these skills supports the automatic processing of printed symbols, which results in fluent reading, thus affording readers the time and energy they need to satisfactorily construct meaning with print. Consequently, the techniques teachers use to develop print processing should assist readers in attaining a set of strategies for the rapid and accurate processing of printed symbols for the purpose of fluent reading.

Our intent in this chapter is to familiarize you with a number of teaching techniques that develop children's print processing strategies. Since print processing does not occur in isolation from actual reading of continuous text, the techniques are presented within the context of broader reading activities and experiences.

In particular, you will examine nine case studies of teachers at work with students as they learn how to process print. The cases permit you to not only watch teachers' techniques, but also to observe how they think about their teaching actions during and after instruction. This deliberate reflection is an important way in which teachers analyze the effectiveness of their teaching and make instructional adjustments (Schön, 1987).

In sum, the cases present three important ideas. First, they highlight that teaching techniques for developing print processing should be embedded in the larger framework of reading instruction. Because the primary reason for reading is comprehension, print processing should support this goal and not be treated as an end unto itself. In other words, learning how to use the skills of print processing should not rob reading of meaning, but rather should contribute to the overall experience.

Second, the cases describe how various teaching techniques may support and extend readers' print processing strategies, that is, how readers can successfully use their language systems to decipher print. In this respect, the techniques serve as clear examples of strategies readers can use while reading on their own.

And finally, the cases illustrate an important phase of the diagnostic process that we discussed in Chapter Two, namely, that as teachers teach, they also reflect, thinking about their decisions and making instructional adjustments as needed. In reading each case, pay particular attention to how these veteran teachers reflect as they teach, remaining alert to children's reading strengths and needs.

As you read each case study, you will analyze what the teacher does, within the framework of the reading lesson, to focus children's attention on words and the skills associated with recalling and deciphering them. In short, you will scrutinize the teaching technique. Then you will summarize it as a strategy, or the "know-how" the reader is developing by participating in the teaching-learning interaction. As a result of your analysis, you will construct a Handbook of Teaching Techniques for Print Processing, which may serve as a resource for you in your own classroom.

Teaching techniques for developing print processing should be embedded in the larger framework of reading instruction.

ACTIVITY 4.1   **A Handbook of Teaching Techniques for Print Processing**
(*Note:* Try this activity with a partner.)

What to Do: Think back to our discussion of analysis in Chapter Two. We said there that analysis is a mental activity that involves "taking things apart" and examining each part, considering how the parts relate to one another and to the whole. That's what you will do in this activity: Take apart what each teacher is doing to examine how print processing is taught so that readers can develop appropriate and useful strategies to use independently. Note how the different parts of each technique relate to one another and to the overall goal of reading—meaning-making. In each case study, you will do the same thing:

1. Read the case study carefully.
2. Reread to analyze the teacher's actions. Examine the teaching technique he or she employs to demonstrate print processing. What is the purpose of the technique—to develop sight-word knowledge, to model word attack, to teach sound-symbol relationships? What is the procedure for the technique? In other words, what did the teacher do *before, during,* and *after* reading to set up or model the technique and to provide the children with an opportunity to practice? In short, analyze the teacher's teaching, noting quite specifically what he or she does.
3. Record your analysis on the technique profile form.
4. Summarize your findings in the form of a reader strategy, using the cloze passage to assist you in your summarization.
5. At some point, compile your technique profiles into your handbook to use in your own classroom teaching.

We encourage you to work with a partner on this activity, since it involves considerable background knowledge about reading as well as attention to detail. Use what you know collectively about learning words based on your experiences as readers and from previous coursework in reading. In bringing this knowledge to bear on each case, you will discover teaching techniques that develop print processing abilities.

Case Study A:
Robert Uses a Language-Experience Technique

Robert had just taken his students for a walk in a nearby woods. He wanted them to record their experiences so he could use the story as a way to teach them to read. In groups of three, he asked them to discuss the things that happened on their walk. After a few minutes, on the chalkboard he generated a master list of some of their remembrances. Next he asked students to tell about their walk, beginning from when they entered the woods.

The children eagerly told about their experiences earlier that day, with details about the setting, including the beautiful wild flowers. They told how they walked on a log across the creek. One of the students fell in the water, which was a problem, but they returned to an open meadow and rested in the sun to allow him to dry off.

As they told the story, Robert wrote the story on a large chart tablet in the front of the room. He often repeated the sentences, asking, "Is this what you said?" This helped the students review how they wanted their story, but it also helped them focus on the words. After they had finished, Robert read the story aloud, again asking the students to join him. He asked them to close their eyes for a minute and think about their walk in the woods. After a few minutes, he began to read the story aloud again.

Next, he said, "Let's read this as if we were grandparents telling our grandchildren about our childhood days." The students followed Robert's finger along the lines of print as they read along in quivering voices. "That was wonderful!" Robert said. "Now let's read it one more time in our normal voices." Again he used his finger, running it along the lines of print as students read in unison.

Robert copied the story onto writing paper that had space for pictures at the top of the pages. He made copies for every student in his class. The next day, he reviewed the story, with all the students reading it in unison. Then he handed out the pages and asked students to practice reading the story with a partner, and to draw pictures about their story. As they did this, Robert listened to each student individually read the story. Most of the students read the story fluently, recognizing the words in the story. When a student stumbled, Robert would say, "Remember what we said about our walk? We said Jimmy fell off the . . ."

Technique Profile: Language-Experience Approach

Purpose Specific to Print Processing:

Procedure

Before reading

During reading

After reading

Reader Strategy Developed

When Robert used the language-experience approach, the students learned new

_____ because they associated their _____ on the

walk and the language they used to _____ the walk with the

_____ on the printed page. As they predicted what the words were, they used

their knowledge of the situation to develop their ability to recognize _____ on

sight and to use their _____ system.

Case Study B:
Brenda Uses Shared Reading

Brenda is working with a group of young readers and decides to use shared reading with the "read to, read with, and you read" sequence. She has chosen the predictable book *Are You My Mother?* by P.D. Eastman (1960). She reads the entire book aloud to her group of students, stopping occasionally to allow them to predict what might happen next.

After they are finished, they discuss the story and Brenda writes on the chalkboard the names of the animals that the young bird meets and the objects that he sees. Next, she reads the book aloud again, letting the students chime in as she reads the repetitious phrases of the book.

Soon the children are reading these phrases alone while Brenda phases back in to complete the less repetitious phrases. After several readings, the students write their own predictable story following the pattern of *Are You My Mother?* This new book is entitled *Are You My Brother?*

As the students are illustrating their new book, Brenda asks each student to read *Are You My Mother?* to her. As they read, she prompts them by asking them what makes sense in the story and what fits in the phrase about the young bird. Sometimes, she prompts the student by asking her/him to look at the picture and then asking, "What animal is that? Is it the young bird's mother?" If the student cannot predict the word, Brenda rereads the sentence, pointing to the unknown word within the context of the story pattern and to the pictures on the page, and thus helps the student figure out the word.

Technique Profile: Shared Reading Approach (Predictable Language)

Purpose Specific to Print Processing:

Procedure

Before reading

During reading

After reading

Reader Strategy Developed

When Brenda used the shared reading experience, the students predicted what the

_____ were by using their knowledge of familiar language patterns and of how

language _____. As they wrote their new story, they focused on the patterns of

_____ in words, learning to recognize the printed form of words that fit the

pattern.

Case Study C:
Chris Uses Message Writing

Chris shows Jennifer a blank writing book and asks Jennifer to think of something she wants to say to a friend. Chris explains to Jennifer that her message will be written on the bottom part of the page. The top of the page is where they will figure out how to write the words that she doesn't know for sure.

Jennifer begins to write the message, slowly saying the words in order to predict the letters in the words. She is able to write the first two or three words, but when she comes to the word *alligator,* she gets stuck. Chris directs her attention to the top of the page, and makes a small box for every letter in the word *alligator.* Then he asks Jennifer to put the letters she knows in the boxes. Jennifer puts an *a* and *l* in the first boxes, and an *r* in the last box.

Chris slowly leads her through the thinking process for determining the unfamiliar letters, asking her to make predictions about each letter and then confirm her guesses by saying the word slowly to hear each sound. When Jennifer does not know what letter to put down, Chris tells her the correct letter, articulating the sound-symbol relationship.

In this way Jennifer begins to think about how words are formed. Chris and Jennifer talk about the letters they filled in the boxes. When they finish writing the word *alligator,* Jennifer writes it in her message. When Jennifer finishes writing the entire message, she reads it aloud to Chris. He says her message is very interesting!

Technique Profile: Message Writing

Purpose Specific to Print Processing:

Procedure

Before reading

During reading

After reading

Reader Strategy Developed

When Chris used the message writing approach, Jennifer predicted what the _____ were using her knowledge of letter-sound patterns in words. As Jennifer predicted the letters in words, she attended to sound-symbol relationships. She is developing her knowledge of the _____ system.

Case Study D:
Sharon Uses Choral Reading

Sharon wanted her students to develop more fluent reading, so she selected a Halloween poem, "This is Halloween" by Dorothy Thompson (1966), for them to practice.

She read the Halloween poem aloud to the class and discussed the meaning as well as how she read it. What parts did she read loudly and what parts did she read softly? Did she read quickly or slowly? What parts did she read in a high voice and what parts did she read in a low voice?

Having numbered each line of the poem, she assigned groups of students a particular line of the poem. The children could easily remember their line because each line started with a different Halloween character, like a ghost, witch, and so on. Most lines had two students reading along with the teacher. Everyone said the last line together: "This is Halloween!"

Sharon read the poem one more time, having the children note their respective parts as well as how she read the part. Then the students practiced their parts in pairs. Finally Sharon and the children read the poem, together.

After they practiced a couple of times, Sharon added accompanying gestures to the poem. The next day she followed the same procedure with a poem from Shel Silverstein's *Where the Sidewalk Ends* (1974).

Technique Profile: Choral Reading

Purpose Specific to Print Processing:

Procedure

Before reading

During reading

After reading

Reader Strategy Developed

When Sharon used the choral reading activity, the students predicted what the _____ were, using their knowledge of the poem and how it was read. As they read the poem, they attended to _____ the words and developed an awareness of how rhythmic reading influences meaning. They also practiced _____ their use of cueing systems, since reading the words relied on using word meaning, sentence sense, and sound-symbol matching.

Case Study E:
David Uses a Retrospective Repeated Reading

David is working with Gary to help him become more fluent and also to help him figure out unfamiliar words as he reads. David has selected the book *Too Much Noise* by Ann McGovern (1967). Before he began the lesson, David made a copy of the first pages of the book and prepared a repeated reading chart like that shown in Figure 4.1.

He introduces the book to Gary by having him look at the pictures and read the title. They discuss what the story might be about. Then, David asks Gary to read the first 70 words of the story aloud, while David marks his copy as he would during an informal reading inventory; he also notes Gary's fluency.

After Gary finishes reading these 70 words, David reviews the miscues with Gary. He selects key miscues to model the self-correcting strategies that proficient readers use. For example, Gary said *house* instead of *horse* in the story. David says, "If I were reading and I made this mistake, I would say to myself, 'Oops, that doesn't make sense. What would make sense and start with a *h?*' " Then, David asks Gary to reread that sentence, using the initial consonant and sentence sense to predict the unknown word.

For other miscues, David simply reads the sentence out loud and has Gary repeat it. After he finishes reviewing the miscues, David asks Gary to read the 70 words again. David uses a different color of pen to mark the miscues made during the second reading. This way they can easily compare the two readings.

After the second reading, David shows Gary how he made fewer mistakes and was using his knowledge of the story to help himself correct miscues. David then puts the number of miscues for the first and second readings on the chart as shown in Figure 4.1.

They discuss how self-correcting can improve reading and understanding as well as how reading something twice can help understanding. Then David asks Gary to review the selection silently. Afterward, Gary reads the selection a third time as David marks miscues and notes fluency, using a fluency rating. After the third reading, they compare miscues and fluency and set goals for the next session. They end by predicting what the next section of the story will be about.

Each day, Gary reads another 70 words of the story. As the repetitive pattern of the story occurs, Gary makes fewer miscues on the initial reading. David and Gary discuss how knowing more about the story helps the reader correct miscues and figure out more difficult words. It is easier to answer the question, "What word would make sense in the story?"

FIGURE 4.1
Repeated reading chart

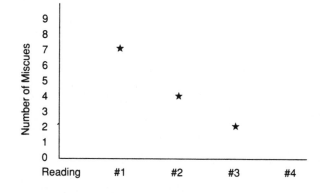

Technique Profile: Retrospective Repeated Reading

Purpose Specific to Print Processing:

Procedure

Before reading

During reading

After reading

Reader Strategy Developed

When David used the retrospective repeated reading technique, he was teaching Gary to use his language _____ and his knowledge of story _____ to correct miscues he had made. In particular, he guided Gary to focus on using multiple cueing systems to decipher troublesome words. That is, he helped Gary to _____ print, using his _____ system, his syntactic system, and his _____ system. Additionally, he demonstrated how to do what _____ readers do when they encounter unknown words.

Case Study F:
Randy Uses Predict and Confirm

Randy wanted his students to be able to use context and their knowledge of letter names to predict unknown words. He decided to make this learning situation a game where he would model the process for a while, and then have other children lead the class. He used the game "Gugglefunk" along with a portion of the text from the trade book *Love You Forever* by Robert Munsch (1990). On the chalkboard, Randy wrote:

He grew until he was nine years old. And he never wanted to come in for

_____ , he never wanted to take a bath, and when grandma

_____ he always said bad words.

As Randy read the text aloud to the children, he said "Gugglefunk" whenever he came to a blank space. Then he asked the children to predict what would go in each blank and he wrote their responses on the chalkboard. He supported probable guesses with comments like, "Yes, that would make sense!"

Next came the fun part. Randy gave the students a clue by telling them that the word for the first blank began with a *d*. Then he wrote the letter in the blank on the chalkboard. Immediately, several children guessed the word *dinner* and Randy wrote it in the blank. With the next blank, Randy continued the process. After telling the children the word began with *v*, he said, "It has three syllables." Then he clapped his hands three times. Then he said, "The first syllable is *vi*," and he pronounced the short *i* sound. Randy wrote the word *visited* in the blank once students suggested it.

Randy emphasized that unfamiliar words can often be figured out by predicting what would make sense in the sentence, and then checking the letters in the words, particularly the first letter.

Technique Profile: Predict and Confirm

Purpose Specific to Print Processing:

Procedure

Before reading

During reading

After reading

Reader Strategy Developed

When Randy used the predict and confirm game, the students predicted what the

_____ were using what would make sense in the sentence; then they confirmed

this by _____ at the letters in the words. As they checked the letters in

words, they attended to the first letter and the word meaning simultaneously. Randy was

developing their knowledge of how to _____ the cueing systems.

Case Study G:
Juanita Uses the Direct Reading Activity

Juanita is working with a group of young readers and has chosen a story from a basal reader. Before reading the story, she introduces unfamiliar words and talks about their structure and meaning. As she does this, she asks students to discuss what they already know about these words.

After Juanita quickly reviews the list of words on the board, she asks students to look at the pictures in the story along with the words on the board and then predict what the story might be about. After a short discussion, she sets a purpose for reading the story. This purpose is more global than specific, designed to engage the students throughout their reading of the story.

She tells the students to read two pages, and then stops to discuss the story up to that point. Juanita restates the purpose for reading the story, elaborating the original purpose with information the students have generated during the discussion. The group continues reading in this manner.

After the story is completed, they discuss the entire story, answering inferential questions. Juanita has students support their discussion by reading aloud parts of the story that influenced their conclusions. If a student has difficulty reading a section aloud, Juanita prompts by saying, "Look at the word. What letter does the word start with? What word do you know that starts with that letter and would mean _____ ?" Finally, they relate the story to their own experiences as well as to other stories they have read.

After the discussion, Juanita reviews the unfamiliar words from the story. She takes the list from the teacher's manual and adds any words that were found to be unfamiliar during the discussion.

Technique Profile: Directed Reading Activity

Purpose Specific to Print Processing:

Procedure

Before reading

During reading

After reading

Reader Strategy Developed

When Juanita used the directed reading activity, the students used their memories for what

the words _____ like. They particularly focused on the initial _____

and the word length, as well as what the word meant. As they came to the new word in the

story, they thought about the words that Juanita had _____ them, attempting

to recall them at _____ .

Case Study H:
Sarah Uses a Word Sort

Each day, Sarah's students make word cards of interesting words that they did not immediately recognize while reading. Some days they get these words from the language-experience stories they wrote; other days they select words from the basal reader or trade book they were reading. Each student has a box of these personalized word cards.

To begin the word sort, Sarah asks the students to get out their word boxes and to get in their cooperative learning groups. She shows them four word cards that she has selected, which contain the words *red, blue, yellow,* and *green.* Then she says, "Why do you think these words go together?"

The students chime in, "They are colors."

"Yes, that one was fairly easy. Now see if you can tell me how these word cards are alike." She shows them *green, grass,* and *grow.* The students respond that all the words start with *gr.* Then Sarah says, "That was more difficult, so I think now you are ready to work on your own. I want you to arrange several word cards that go together in some way. Then, read your words to your group and see if anyone in your group can guess why you arranged the words together." The students use many different ways to group the words. Some use letter-sound relationships, some use the meanings of the words, and some use how the words are used in a sentence, like *has, have, had.*

Sarah gives the students time to complete a couple of word sorts in this fashion (open word sort). Then she decides to direct their attention to letter patterns. She asks them to look at their word banks and select words that follow the same letter pattern at the end of the word. Each student looks through his or her word bank, looking for letter patterns in much the same way as a reader mentally sorts through known words to find a pattern similar to an unfamiliar word. When the students find several words, they share their words in their groups and tell how the words are alike.

The next day, Sarah has a set of word cards for each cooperative learning group. These word cards have letter patterns that are somewhat similar, for example, *le* at the end of the words, as in *bottle.* The group is to arrange the cards according to the letter pattern. Sarah gives the students time to complete this word sort (closed word sort), and then asks the students to tell how the words are alike.

Technique Profile: Word Sort

Purpose Specific to Print Processing:

Procedure

Before reading

During reading

After reading

Reader Strategy Developed

When Sarah used the word sort activities, the students looked for ways their words could

be _____ together. They used their sight-word knowledge along with their

ability to categorize information based on either their meaning (semantic cues) or their

_____ similarity (graphophonemic cues). As they sorted their cards, they

focused on how words are _____ , a mental activity used in everyday life. When

Sarah used the closed sort, she helped the students look for letter _____

in words they already knew. This helped them develop the process of decoding by analogy.

Case Study I:
Bobbi Uses the Cloze Activity

Bobbi has developed a cloze activity using a favorite part of the story *Freckle Juice* by Judy Blume (1971). She deletes every seventh word from two paragraphs; however, she leaves the initial letter of the deleted word intact. She asks Jerry to fill in the blanks. As Jerry completes the cloze activity, he thinks about the words around the blank and thinks about what word would fit in the sentence. In doing so, he uses his knowledge of sentence patterns and sound-symbol relationships to figure out words in sentences.

Technique Profile: Cloze Activity

Purpose Specific to Print Processing:

Procedure

Before reading

During reading

After reading

Reader Strategy Developed

When Bobbi used the cloze activity, the students predicted what the _____ were

using their knowledge of sentence patterns. As they predicted the words, they attended

to how syntax influences word choices. They are developing their knowledge of

the _____ system.

FOLLOW-UP DISCUSSION

Print processing involves the orchestration of the reader's language systems.

From language experience to choral reading, the teaching techniques for developing print processing reinforce two main ideas we began with in this chapter, namely, that teaching children about words should be embedded in meaningful reading experiences and that print processing is the *orchestration* of the readers' language systems. Although the nine technique profiles you have just completed represent only a small number of teaching techniques available for fostering readers' print processing, they are some of the most commonly used and some of the most effective. We encourage you to include additional techniques as you come across them in your own teaching.

Too often teachers fail to make changes in instruction because they are unaware of instructional techniques and how these techniques can help. Your handbook serves not only as an immediate resource, but also as a constant reminder that your acquisition of teaching techniques for print processing should be ongoing if you are to assist children in this aspect of the reading process. You need to build a collection of print processing teaching techniques that support and enhance your instructional decision making.

Knowing about these nine teaching techniques, however, is not enough. You must also be aware of how each technique furthers the reading process if you are to make informed instructional decisions about their use. Therefore, in the next activity, we invite you to organize them (and future ones) in a way that reflects the problem-solving nature of the reading process.

Once again, recall the psycholinguistic model of reading discussed in Chapter One, thinking about its predicting, confirming, and integrating elements. Then, think about how the teaching techniques in this chapter help students to use these behaviors when learning how to process the printed word. As you engage in this project, you will organize the techniques in an efficient way for later instructional use, and you also will reflect about their purposes, providing rationales for that instruction.

ACTIVITY 4.2   **Creating a Matrix of Print Processing Techniques**
(*Note:* Do this with a partner or in a small group.)

What to Do: To organize teaching techniques for print processing, you will make a matrix or grid that sorts them according to the particular processes they each foster. The format for the matrix is provided. Note that three key processes reflective of the overall reading process are written across the top of the matrix.

List all the teaching techniques you examined in the chapter. Then evaluate (judge) each technique, assigning it to the process you think it stresses. Ask yourself: Does this technique primarily develop children's abilities, using print cues, to make predictions? Or does it especially encourage children to confirm their predictions, using print cues and word meaning? Or does it lead to the elaboration of word knowledge? Or does it tend to enhance all three of these processes simultaneously?

An open word sort, for example, encourages children to categorize words in new ways and thus elaborate their knowledge of word features. The language-experience approach, on the other hand, seems to focus on children's predicting abilities, prompting them to guess at new words and to apply their language systems in deciphering the words as they read.

Somewhat more challenging, this activity deepens your knowledge of the nine teaching techniques presented in Activity 4.1, increasing your familiarity with them and thereby the likelihood of their use in your own teaching. As you learn about additional teaching techniques for developing children's print processing strategies, add them to your matrix, evaluating them as well. To illustrate what to do, in the matrix we have indicated our evaluation of the two techniques we just cited.

Teaching Techniques	*Processes*		
	Prediction	*Confirmation*	*Elaboration*
Language-Experience Approach	*		
Open Word Sort			*

FOLLOW-UP DISCUSSION

This analysis and evaluation of the nine teaching techniques will help you in selecting an appropriate instructional technique when you are teaching print processing. If we are to develop readers who can successfully use the reading process, then it is critical that we think about and reflect on how the various techniques we choose lead children to increasing control of it.

Now, as we have done before, it is time to connect what you have studied with the real thing, that is, real readers and writers. Knowledge of different teaching techniques is best developed through the actual use of each and every one. In other words, to know it is to do it. So, the final activity engages you in trying out a technique or two with a living, breathing, thinking reader.

As important as this practice is, however, reflecting on it is just as important. Consequently, in the activity we urge you to try out a technique and then to rethink what you did, constructing a rationale for your actions. For example, ask yourself: What did this teaching technique accomplish with respect to the child's ability to process print more effectively? Although sometimes difficult to answer quickly, such self-questioning and reflection are essential if we are to teach so that children learn.

| **ACTIVITY 4.3** | **Practicing Print Processing Teaching Techniques** |

(*Note:* Try this activity with a developing reader.)

What to Do: In this activity, you will practice one of the nine print processing techniques. Choose one and schedule time to use the instructional technique with a young reader. Keep a log of your teaching. In addition to the name and age of the reader you assisted, each entry should include the technique you used, a summary of what you did, and a self-evaluation. A sample format for your entry is provided.

Sample Entry Form

Child's Name: Age:

Date: Technique:

Summary of Procedures:

Self-Evaluation:

Summary

Although Alice in Wonderland was advised, "take care of the sense and the sounds will take care of themselves," this is not exactly the case. Readers *do* benefit from instruction that develops their abilities to process print. Just as students actively construct understanding, they need to know how to actively figure out what words are. This is print processing.

The case studies in this chapter and the profiles accompanying them have given you opportunities to understand and use instructional techniques that support and extend children's print processing know-how. Some of these techniques are: a language-experience approach, a sight-word approach, word sorts, shared reading, repeated readings, message writing, predict/confirm activity, the cloze activity, and choral reading. As you participated in the chapter's activities, you began to compile a Handbook of Teaching Techniques—a resource you will undoubtedly augment as you continue your study of reading instruction. You also evaluated the techniques, constructing a matrix based on the essential elements of the reading process. Finally, you tried some of the techniques on your own with a young reader, practicing your skill at teaching print processing.

Further Reading

Gillet, J. W., & Temple, C. (1990). *Understanding Reading Problems* (3rd ed.). Glenview, IL: Scott-Foresman. This book presents numerous techniques to support children who have difficulty reading. It includes a chapter on corrective teaching techniques, including developing sight-word vocabulary, reading fluency, and word analysis.

Tierney, R. J., Readence, J. E., & Dishner, E. K. (1990). *Reading strategies and practices: A compendium* (3rd ed.). Boston: Allyn & Bacon. This book contains a series of chapters devoted to explaining teaching techniques for meaning and print processing. Each technique is thoroughly explained according to its theoretical and research base, as well as how it has been implemented in classrooms.

Walker, Barbara J. (1992). *Diagnostic teaching of reading: Techniques for instruction and assessment* (2nd ed.). New York: Merrill/Macmillan. This book presents numerous techniques for developing print processing strategies. The teaching techniques are outlined in sequential steps with an accompanying description including predominant focus of instruction and how to use reader strengths.

CHAPTER FIVE

◆

Teaching Techniques and Reader Strategies for Meaning Processing

◆

We had the experience, but missed the meaning.
—T.S. Eliot

Let's return once again to the psycholinguistic model of the reading process discussed in Chapter One. In this model, readers actively construct meaning as they think about the author's message. They are engaged, so to speak, in negotiating meaning with the author. We refer to this as **meaning processing,** or how readers comprehend the author's message.

Meaning processing involves readers in making predictions about content and then confirming those predictions using the text (which actually "represents" the author) while simultaneously integrating the author's message with what they already know. The intensity of this mental activity requires active participation with the text to make the overall reading experience informative and satisfying. Readers must actively predict, monitor, and elaborate what they are reading, synthesizing important information and interlinking it with their schemata.

Sometimes, however, students miss the author's intended meaning because they concentrate more on pronouncing words (processing print) rather than on weaving the text into a comprehensible whole (meaning processing), leading them to say, "I read it, but I don't get it." Since merely reading words is not reading, students must learn to process print and meaning simultaneously if reading is to be meaningful and enjoyable. Consequently, students need guidance in how to process text at a deeper level by constructing meaning with the printed symbols they are deciphering.

Constructing meaning encompasses the traditional instructional areas of vocabulary development, literal and nonliteral comprehension, use of text structure as an aid to comprehension, questioning and inferencing strategies, and figurative language (e.g., metaphor and imagery). In short, it is all the behaviors, factors, and qualities that readers bring to written language which aid them in understanding and appreciating the author's message.

Certain teaching techniques and reader strategies used before, during, and after reading can greatly facilitate students' abilities to process meaning. In this chapter, we will present nine teaching techniques that teach children how to process meaning so that they can use these strategies on their own while reading. We call these techniques "bread and butter" techniques, because they can be used, and probably should be used, consistently and regularly in reading instruction.

As done in the last chapter on print processing, in this chapter you will examine case studies of teachers at work supporting and guiding students' awareness and use of meaning processing strategies. Like print processing, the development

Readers must actively predict, monitor, and elaborate what they are reading, synthesizing important information and interlinking it with their schemata.

of meaning processing does not occur in isolation, but rather within the context of a whole reading experience. Through the case studies, you will have an opportunity to organize, for your own use, procedures for teaching meaning processing.

In addition, the activities in this chapter will further your understanding that teaching techniques that develop meaning processing (a) need to be an integral part of all reading instruction and should be linked with the teaching of print processing; (b) need to develop students' abilities to process text at a deeper level beyond the mere reading of words; (c) should guide students in the ability to use strategies with texts—to make predictions about the forthcoming information, to confirm their predictions by using the text content as well as their own knowledge, and to connect the author's message to their own lives; and (d) must be continually evaluated—as teachers teach, they need to reflect about their instructional decisions, considering the effectiveness and appropriateness of their instruction for enhancing readers' processes and skills.

As you study each case, analyze what the teacher does within the framework of the reading lesson to focus children's attention on comprehending the text. Following this step, summarize your findings in the form of a strategy, that is, the "know-how" the reader is developing by participating in the teaching-learning interaction. Based on your analyses of the nine cases, you will construct a Handbook of Teaching Techniques for Meaning Processing, which will serve as a resource in your own instructional work.

| ACTIVITY 5.1 | **A Handbook of Teaching Techniques for Meaning Processing** |

(*Note:* Try this activity with a partner.)

What to Do: Recall how you analyzed the case studies in Chapter Four, describing print processing teaching techniques. Similarly, to ascertain how meaning processing is taught so that readers can use these strategies on their own, you will also take apart what the teachers are doing.

For each case study:

1. Read the case study carefully.
2. Reread to analyze the teacher's actions. Examine the teaching technique he or she employs to demonstrate meaning processing. What is the central purpose of the technique: to develop vocabulary, to present text structure as an aid to comprehension, to enhance students' abilities to summarize what they have read, or to encourage inference-making while reading? What is the procedure for the technique? In other words, what did the teacher do before, during, and after reading to set up, to model the technique, and to provide the children with an opportunity to practice? In short, analyze the teacher's teaching, noting quite specifically what he or she does.
3. Record your analysis on the Technique Profile form.
4. Summarize your findings in the form of a reader strategy, using the cloze passage to assist you in your summarization.
5. At some point, compile your technique profiles into your handbook for use in your own classroom teaching.

If you found that working with a partner was beneficial in constructing your Handbook of Teaching Techniques for Print Processing, we encourage you to do the same here. Once again, rely on what you already know about comprehension based on your experiences as a reader and on previous coursework. In combining this knowledge with your observations of the teachers in the cases, you will discover a number of useful techniques for teaching meaning processing.

Case Study A:
Carmen Uses the Directed Reading-Thinking Activity

Carmen is working with a group of young readers, using the trade book *Sam, Bangs, and Moonshine* by Eveline Ness (1966). Carmen introduces the story by reviewing the pictures and asking the students what they believe the story will be about. She writes their guesses on the chalkboard.

The students then read the first two pages, and Carmen asks them what happened. She reviews with them their predictions and asks if they want to keep, add to, or change them. As she discusses their predictions and revisions with them, she asks them to justify their decisions. Next, she has the students predict how Sam will solve her problem. She writes these guesses on the board.

Carmen has students continue reading to the point where the storm covers Blue Rock. Then, she discusses the story so far and again reviews predictions, asking students if they want to keep or discard them. She asks for justifications of their predictions, based on both the text and the children's experiences. Then she solicits new predictions. The students finish reading the story. After they read the story, they discuss Sam's problems and how she solved them.

Finally, Carmen asks students how they figured out the story. She reviews the number of predictions they made and how their guesses were closer to the actual text at each point in the story. She discusses how the information in the story and what they already knew about similar situations helped them understand Sam.

Technique Profile: Directed Reading-Thinking Activity

Purpose Specific to Meaning Processing:

Procedure

Before reading

During reading

After reading

Reader Strategy Developed

As Carmen taught using the directed reading-thinking activity, the students learned

to _____ what might happen in the story. By asking them to

_____ their predictions, the students also began to share how they were

thinking, including their similar experiences. Additionally, the sharing of their various

_____ for the story helped the students

_____ and elaborate their story comprehension.

Case Study B:
Steve Uses a Story Frame

Steve is working with a group of young readers, using the trade book *The Little Red Hen* (Galdone, 1975). Steve introduces the story by reviewing the pictures and asking the students what they believe the story will be about. Then, he reminds them that in stories, main characters have problems to solve. The characters develop a plan to solve the problem and then resolve it.

The students read the first two pages, and Steve asks them who the main character is and what her problem is. He writes this information on a story frame that he has placed on the board, similar to the following:

This story takes place _____ . The main character in the story,

_____ has a problem. The problem starts when _____ .

After that, _____ . Next, _____ . The problem was

solved when _____ . The story ends when _____ .

Next, Steve has the students predict how the little red hen will solve her problem. Then the students finish reading the story. After they read the story, they discuss the little red hen's problem and how she solved the problem, completing the story frame. They discuss how successful the little red hen really was at solving the problem. Then, on their own story frames, they organize the key events that led to the resolution.

Finally, Steve asks the students to retell the story to their neighbor, using their story frames as memory prompts. The next day, Steve has them write a summary of *The Little Red Hen* on their own.

Technique Profile: Story Frames

Purpose Specific to Meaning Processing:

Procedure

Before reading

During reading

After reading

Reader Strategy Developed

When Steve used the story frame, he asked the students to think about how a

_____ is constructed. By focusing on the story parts, the students could

_____ what was going to happen by thinking about what part of the story

would come next. As they retold and wrote about the story, they used their knowledge of

story _____ to help them recall and comprehend the essential mean-

ing of the story.

Case Study C:
Dana Uses Retellings

Dana wants her students to be able to retell a story that represents not only what the author said, but also what students' own personal interpretations of the story are. To select stories, Dana lets each student choose a trade book from the five she has placed in front of the class. To begin, she gives a brief highlight of each book and has students select their books. As each student finishes reading, she invites him or her to her desk to retell the story. As each student retells, she notes what is included, how information is organized, and what personal interpretations are related, using the form provided in Figure 5.1.

If the student is hesitant, Dana encourages him or her to continue, using prompts such as, "Who are the characters?" or "What happened to _____ in the story?" She becomes more supportive and directive if the student is totally unable to retell the story.

After each child finishes the retelling, Dana chats with him or her, querying about likes and dislikes, as well as about information omitted in the retelling. She uses her notes to double-check the student's retelling and personal interpretations.

FIGURE 5.1
Retelling guide

Quick Form: Impressions of a Retelling

Features	Impressions		
	No 1	*Partial* 2	*Yes* 3
1. Expresses the main idea	|------------------|	------------------ |
2. Mentions sufficient detail	|------------------|	------------------ |
3. Logically structures retelling	|------------------|	------------------ |
4. Infers from text	|------------------|	------------------ |
5. Connects to other experiences	|------------------|	------------------ |

Score: _____

Technique Profile: Retellings

Purpose Specific to Meaning Processing:

Procedure

Before reading

During reading

After reading

Reader Strategy Developed

When Dana used retellings, he asked the students to relate their understanding of a

story. Through this recall experience, students had to use their knowledge of story

_____ as well as how a story is organized, or its _____ .

As they retold, they revealed the extent of their _____ and

their personal _____ of the story.

Case Study D:
Kyle Uses ReQuest (Reciprocal Questioning) (Manzo, 1969)

Kyle wants his students to be more active in their approach to stories. He chooses an ambiguous mystery story from the *Encyclopedia Brown* series by Sobol (*Encyclopedia Brown Takes a Case,* 1973).

He begins by asking students to look at the title and then to ask him a question. After answering their questions, he asks them a question. This turn-taking between teacher and students continues as they read the next few paragraphs of the text.

The students read the first paragraph silently. They ask Kyle questions. Then he asks them a question, making sure he asks one that can be answered in the context of the paragraph. For example, where is this story taking place?

They jointly read the next paragraph. The students again ask Kyle questions, and again Kyle answers the questions, elaborating his responses with information from the first two paragraphs and from what he knows about *Encyclopedia Brown* mysteries, thus modelling higher order thinking. He then asks a higher order evaluative question, like "Using evidence from the story, what would you do if you were in the same situation as Encyclopedia Brown?" Kyle and his students continue alternating like this for another two paragraphs. Then the students finish reading the story on their own. Afterwards, Kyle and his students discuss the story at some length.

Technique Profile: ReQuest (Reciprocal Questioning)

Purpose Specific to Meaning Processing:

Procedure

Before reading

During reading

After reading

Reader Strategy Developed

As the students asked Kyle _____ , they had to think about the important information in the selection. As the story progressed, their questions revealed their _____ and how they _____ the information together. This question-asking behavior enhanced their stance toward meaning processing because they thought about important information and _____ how the story was proceeding so they could ask good questions.

Case Study E:
Connie Uses Self-directed Questioning (Walker, 1992a)

Connie wants her students to monitor their reading, using both what they are reading and what they know about what they are reading. She selects the story *Two Were Left* (Cave, 1989), because students must naturally change their predictions as they read more of the story. She carefully divides this story at critical points where students will be uncertain about the outcome and will, perhaps, change or add to their predictions.

As Connie begins, she models the self-questioning process using a short story from *More Scary Stories to Tell in the Dark* (Schwartz, 1984) that she has reproduced and placed on an overhead. She presents the title and models making a prediction by saying, "When I begin to read, I make predictions or bets about the story." Then she writes the words, "I bet" on the board and makes her bet.

I bet that . . .

She presents the second section of the story and models confirming her bet, using what she already knows about the text. Then she adds to the I-bet statement.

The text says . . .   I already knew. . .

She presents the third section of the story and models changing her bet by writing "Oops" on the board and saying, "Sometimes, I make mistakes. When I get more information, I can change my mind. Now I bet. . ."

Oops!

Then she presents the fourth section of the story and models her uncertainty. From the hints in the text, she doesn't really know what will happen. So she adds to the "Oops," a "Hm-m-m."

Oops!   Hm-m-m . . .

Then she presents the fifth section of the story and models her certainty because the text had proved her prediction. She says, "I knew it! My bet was right because the text says . . . and I know that . . ."

I knew it!

After modeling this active process, together the students and teacher read *Two Were Left,* using this process. Again, Connie uses the overhead projector and presents the story in sections, but this time she supports her students as they use the self-directed questions and redirects their thinking with questions like: "What can you tell yourself about your bet?" or "How did you figure out the knife was important?" Following their reading of the story, the students discuss how they revised their predictions as they read the story. They talk about the sources of information they used to construct the meaning of the story.

Technique Profile: Self-directed Questioning

Purpose Specific to Meaning Processing:

Procedure

Before reading

During reading

After reading

Reader Strategy Developed

When Connie used the self-directed questioning, she asked the students to _____

what would happen, using both the text and what they _____ . By focusing on revis-

ing their predictions, the students _____ how their comprehension

was occurring as well as the sources of _____

they were using.

Case Study F:
Tom Uses a Three-Level Guide

Tom wants his students to understand and use social studies concepts; to foster this, he teaches his students three levels of responding to information. To model this he constructs a study guide that asks students to respond to three kinds of questions:

- What did the author say? (literal level of comprehension)
- What did the author mean? (interpretive level of comprehension)
- How does this relate to you or how will you use this? (applied level of comprehension)

Tom carefully goes through the reading selection and notes the main points. He develops statements (not questions) related to the selection at the three levels of comprehension. From this, he constructs a guide.

To begin the lesson, he explains the three levels of comprehension:

When we read, sometimes we want to know *exactly* what the author said. This information is stated 'right there' in the text and we often call these the facts. Sometimes, however, we need to interpret those facts by using information that we already know and tying together several facts from the text. When we do this, we are really interpreting what the author means. In other words, we have to 'think and search,' reading between the lines to figure out what the author means.

Finally, we sometimes simply use the information and the interpretation to build our own ideas about the topic. In other words, we are 'on our own.' When we do this, we are really relating the information to our own knowledge, confirming and expanding what we already know.

Based on the selection we will be reading, I have prepared a study guide that has statements from these three levels of understanding. Beside each statement, mark an *A* if you agree with the statement and a *D* if you disagree. Before you read the selection, skim through all the statements. They will help you define your purpose for reading.

After you finish reading, go through the three-level guide and put a *D* or an *A* by each statement. If you need to, feel free to go back and reread before you make your decision.

Following their completion of the study guides, Tom has the students discuss their responses in a small group, justifying why they agree or disagree with the statements, using the text and their own experiences to support their decisions.

Technique Profile: Three-Level Guide

Purpose Specific to Meaning Processing:

Procedure

Before reading

During reading

After reading

Reader Strategy Developed

As the students completed the study guide, they had to use both _____

information and reader-based information. The study guide directed their active processing

of the text, leading them to agree or disagree with statements that could be facts—informa-

tion "_____ _____" in the text, interpretations that involve

'_____ and _____', or pure opinions that we think

about _____ _____ _____ .

Case Study G:
Marty Uses Semantic Mapping

Marty wants her students to use key words to predict what a passage will be about by using what they know about the topic. She selects key vocabulary words from a passage about volcanoes: *volcano, lava, core.*

She begins with the most general word, *volcano.* She puts this word in the center of a circle on the chalkboard and asks the students what they know about this word. As they brainstorm what they know, Marty draws lines from the circle and organizes the supplied information into categories around the circle.

She begins the discussion with, "What does a volcano do?" She puts students' replies extending from one line. Then she asks them what a volcano is made of, and puts this information extending from another line. She asks if any one knows the parts of the volcano, and puts this information extending from another line. As students suggest information unrelated to the key concepts, Marty puts this information extending from a fourth line. The semantic map looks something like the one shown in Figure 5.2.

After the map is completed, Marty and her students generate questions that they think will be answered by the selection on volcanoes. They read the selection silently. After reading, they return to their semantic map, adding any new information they have learned to the map. Marty then has her students use the map to develop a written summary about volcanoes.

FIGURE 5.2
Example of semantic map

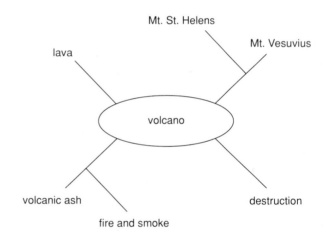

Technique Profile: Semantic Mapping

Purpose Specific to Meaning Processing:

Procedure

Before reading

During reading

After reading

Reader Strategy Developed

By filling out the semantic map _____ they read the story, Marty and her students were able to evaluate what they _____ knew about what they were reading. The students could use this information to help them construct new _____ as they read. Completing the semantic map after reading helped them _____ the new information to concepts they already knew.

Case Study H:
Bryan Uses Graphic Organizers

Bryan wants his students to be able to relate key vocabulary words within a broad conceptual framework, making it easier for students to determine relationships between ideas and to elaborate both known and new concepts. He selects a few key vocabulary words and arranges them into a diagram that illustrates their relationship, for example, general statement and details, cause to effect, or comparison-contrast. Within a graphic organizer format—a sort of "picture" of how the ideas are related in the selection—Bryan uses some familiar vocabulary words as well as new words that his students have been learning. (See Figure 5.3.)

Before students begin reading the chapter, Bryan puts his graphic organizer on the chalkboard and explains the new words and how they are related. He encourages students to give their explanations and to link new vocabulary words to known words.

As they are reading the chapter, Bryan encourages students to refer to the graphic organizer to help them make connections and elaborate the content. They can also jot related words next to vocabulary in the organizer.

After reading, Bryan uses the graphic organizer as a tool for discussion. First, in small groups the students provide rationales for the visual relationships, articulating their growing understanding of new ideas. Then these groups share their rationales and points in a large group discussion.

FIGURE 5.3
Example of a graphic organizer

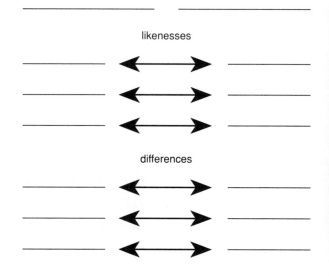

Technique Profile: Graphic Organizers

Purpose Specific to Meaning Processing:

Procedure

Before reading

During reading

After reading

Reader Strategy Developed

By using the graphic organizer, the students made _____

between unfamiliar vocabulary words and the concepts they represented. The students

could use this graphic organizer to help them construct new _____

as they read. Discussing the graphic organizer after reading helped them _____

the new information to concepts they already knew.

Case Study I:
Lynn Uses a Learning Log in Science

Lynn wants her students to be actively involved in science experiments and in reading their textbooks. At the end of every class period, she asks them to write in their science learning logs. They are to write about what they are learning, responding to the following prompts: What Did I Learn Today?, New Words For Me, and Questions I Still Have.

Once a week, Lynn collects the logs and writes responses that encourage the students to continue and to expand their thinking. She asks them to think about experiments related to what they are writing about. She also comments about other projects or reading that relate to the topic being studied. In each entry, she tries to have students connect what they are learning to other things they have discussed.

Technique Profile: Learning Logs

Purpose Specific to Meaning Processing:

Procedure

Before reading

During reading

After reading

Reader Strategy Developed

By writing in a log, the students could _____ on what they were learning. They also could decide for themselves what was important to learn. Lynn's comments encouraged them to extend what they were _____ to other areas and to connect what they were learning to what they already _____ . In other words, the technique helped students to link what they were learning with what they knew.

FOLLOW-UP DISCUSSION

Meaning processing teaching techniques focus on demonstrating how to become engaged with the author's ideas and intentions. The key strategy to be developed, it seems, is how to actively participate in a conversation which is essentially in the head of the reader. Because print cannot "talk back," a heavy demand is placed on the reader to "carry the conversation" and to make sense out of it. This is no easy task for beginning and developing readers who may easily become confused, and thus impatient, with the print (the author). Consequently, meaning processing teaching techniques need to be used frequently and repeatedly. In this activity you have become acquainted with nine such techniques. We encourage you to include them in your Handbook of Teaching Techniques.

As an aside, we have a teacher friend who began to develop a Handbook of Teaching Techniques during her first year of teaching. To date, she has over 100 techniques in her book, which she refers to as her "compendium."

Although not yet a compendium, the Handbook of Teaching Techniques you are compiling may represent the beginning of one for you. We certainly encourage you to continue adding to the Handbook, and at the end of this chapter we provide some resources for other technique ideas.

As we indicated in the last chapter, knowing why you are using these techniques is as important as knowing how. So, in the following activity you will again create a matrix indicating the specific processes each technique attempts to develop.

ACTIVITY 5.2	**Creating a Matrix of Meaning Processing Techniques**

(*Note:* Do this with a partner or a small group.)

What to Do: To organize teaching techniques for meaning processing, in this activity you will make a matrix or grid which sorts them according to the particular processes they each foster. The format for the matrix is provided in the following figure. Note that the three key processes reflective of the overall reading process are written across the top of the matrix.

List all the teaching techniques you examined in the chapter. Then evaluate each technique, assigning it to the process you think it stresses. Ask yourself: Does this technique primarily develop children's ability to make predictions about the content of the author's message? Or does it especially encourage children to confirm their predictions by using text-based information as well as schema-based information? Or does it lead to the elaboration of meaning? Or does it tend to enhance all three of these processes simultaneously?

A Directed Reading-Thinking Activity, for example, encourages children to make predictions and confirm them using text cues. Semantic mapping, on the other hand, seems to focus on children's predicting abilities, prompting them to share what they already know about a particular idea or topic.

Like the challenge presented to you in Chapter Four, this activity deepens your knowledge of the nine teaching techniques presented in this chapter, increasing your familiarity with them and thereby the likelihood that you will use them in your own teaching. As you learn about additional teaching techniques for developing children's meaning processing strategies, add them to your matrix, evaluating them as well. To illustrate what to do, in the matrix we have indicated our evaluation of the two techniques we cited previously.

Matrix of Meaning Processing Techniques

Techniques	Prediction	Confirmation	Elaboration
		Processes	
DR-TA	*	*	
Story Frames	*		*

FOLLOW-UP DISCUSSION	By participating in the activities in these last two chapters, you are becoming increasingly familiar with teaching techniques that you can use to support and extend children's control of the reading process. Moreover, you can become more confident in your ability to select techniques that meet students' needs and further their abilities to problem-solve using written language. Keep in mind that meaning processing and print processing techniques should complement one another within the

larger framework of the reading lesson. Moreover, their overriding purpose is to engage children in reading experiences that are meaningful and satisfying. In short, the techniques are a means to reading achievement, not the end.

By now, however, you are probably eager to try out some of the teaching techniques for meaning processing with real children who are equally as eager (we hope). So, in the final activity you will again practice some techniques with children of your choice. Be alert to your thinking behaviors, as well as to theirs, and be sure to thank them for helping you out.

ACTIVITY 5.3 **Practicing Meaning Processing Teaching Techniques**
(*Note:* Try this activity with a developing reader.)

What to Do: In this activity you will practice two meaning processing instructional techniques, selecting from the nine presented in Activity 5.1.

Choose two techniques and schedule a time to use them with a developing reader. Keep a log of your instructional attempts. In addition to the reader's name and age, each entry should include the technique you used, a summary of what you did, and a self-evaluation. A sample entry form is provided.

Sample Entry Form

Reader's Name: Age:

Date: Technique:

Summary of Procedures:

Self-Evaluation:

Summary

The case studies in this chapter as well as your own experiences have given you opportunities to understand teaching techniques for developing meaning processing strategies. Of the wide array of techniques we use as teachers, those involving meaning processing are probably some of *the* most important. If teaching is to engage children in worthwhile learning experiences, then meaning-making must be at its very core. If lacking, children may do what we ask them to do, but it may not help them to become successful readers.

Students' active construction of meaning allows them to synthesize important information from both the text and what they know. They are making meaning for themselves. The teaching techniques we choose can strengthen and enhance readers' strategies which are so essential for this highly successful use of written language.

Students' active construction of meaning allows them to synthesize important information from both the text and what they know.

Further Reading

Irvin, Judith L. (1990). *Reading and the middle school student: Strategies to enhance literacy.* Boston: Allyn & Bacon. This book has chapters that explain vocabulary, prior knowledge, comprehending, and remembering text. Each of these chapters includes numerous techniques explained in general steps that develop these aspects of meaning processing.

Tierney, R. J., Readence, J. E., & Dishner, E. K. (1990). *Reading strategies and practices: A compendium* (3rd ed.). Boston: Allyn & Bacon. This book contains a series of chapters devoted to explaining teaching techniques for meaning and print processing. Each technique is thoroughly explained according to its theoretical and research base as well as how it may be implemented in the classroom.

Vacca, R., & Vacca, J. (1991). *Content area reading.* Glenview, Ill: Scott, Foresman. Throughout this book a number of reader strategies are described. They are organized into those which may enhance meaning processing before, during, and after reading.

Walker, Barbara J. (1992). *Diagnostic teaching of reading: Techniques for instruction and assessment* (2nd ed.). New York: Merrill/Macmillan. Well-organized, this book presents numerous techniques for developing meaning processing strategies. The teaching techniques are outlined in sequential steps with an accompanying description that includes predominant focus of instruction and reader strengths.

CHAPTER SIX

◆

An Instructional Routine
for Diagnostic Teaching

◆

Routines play such a major role in the teacher's planning behavior that [such] planning could be characterized as decision making about the selection, organization, and sequencing of routines.
—Robert Yinger

So far in our work together we have established a conceptual foundation and become familiar with assessment and instructional techniques. But, even though all the activities you have done so far may have furthered your understanding of diagnosis, you still may feel that you have only bits and pieces of what it means to teach diagnostically—only slices of real-life diagnostic reading instruction. In the back of your mind, you might be wondering: "But, how do I do this every day in a classroom filled with living, breathing, squirming, wiggling children? How do I put diagnosis to work in my teaching?"

As with most things we should do nearly every day, we need an instructional routine—a course of action that includes diagnosis in an easy and natural way. Now, when we use this word *routine,* we are not implying a rigid prescription for instruction that leads to boring teaching habits and ritualized instructional procedures. Rather, we are using the word *routine* in a broad sense, as an instructional route— a teaching pathway that encompasses the processes and procedures of diagnosis. If we are to embed diagnosis in our teaching, an instructional routine is needed that structures learning activities to include diagnosis, yet one that is flexible enough to allow for the "little" things (and inevitably important things) that pop up in our instructional conversations with children.

Drawing from a number of existing instructional frameworks (e.g., Baskwill, 1989; Clay, 1985; Walker, 1992a; Weaver, 1988), we have developed an instructional routine that provides a flexible structure for diagnostic teaching, that is, a structure with enough give to accommodate the press of classroom life. This routine includes six activities that are described in the following section.

An Instructional Routine for Diagnostic Teaching

◆ **Warm Up:**   Warm ups are brief (about three minutes or so), enjoyable encounters with "short, digestible bits of print" (Baskwill, 1989). Just like athletes must warm up before strenuous exercise, readers need to ease into the challenge that print may present. Most successful readers tend to do this in one way or another. For example, they may study the pictures in a text, reading the captions. They may quickly scan pages of print, sizing up the situation. Sometimes readers flip through pages, noting headings and bold print. Students often count pages! All of these are ways to "warm up" to print—a most healthy thing to do.

Teachers need to provide children with warm-up experiences as a regular part of the instructional routine. Reading jokes, writing commercials, sharing journal entries, jotting down impressions of paintings or music, doing magic tricks, or reading rhymes and jingles are all examples of warm ups.

Warm ups can be related to subsequent reading selections or topics of study, but they do not have to be. The important rule is that they are bits of reading and writing that are easy and enjoyable to do. Of course, during warm-up activities, the alert teacher notes children's interests, abilities, and background knowledge.

> Warm ups are bits of reading and writing that are easy and enjoyable and that ease children into reading.

> Familiar texts are selections that children have already read and know well.

◆ **Using Familiar Text:**   Familiar text includes selections and excerpts that children have already read and *know well* (Clay, 1985). These texts may be pieces children have published, or commercial text selections (trade books, content texts, or basals).

At this point in the instructional routine, it is valuable to have children reread something simply because they really like it, for example, an old favorite. The instructional purpose here is sheer fun, which, by the way, does a lot for intrinsic motivation. When teachers provide children with opportunities to reread for the fun of it, they are fostering an internal propensity—a desire—to read which lasts a lifetime.

Familiar text can be effectively used in other ways at different points in the instructional routine, for example, to teach specific skills and processes. At the outset of the reading lesson, however, one of its major benefits is to remind children of what they already know and can do, bolstering their confidence as readers. Consequently, the focus here should be on enjoyment and pleasure—reading favorite poems, picture books, short excerpts from novels, and other information of interest.

> New text is the challenge requiring "cognitive stretch."

◆ **Reading New Text:**   New text is the challenge, requiring "cognitive stretch," or complex cognitive actions on the part of the reader (Cazden, 1981). In this situation, what readers know is "put to the text," so to speak, as a new dialogue is initiated between reader and author. Readers must now apply what they know to new print situations and share with others what they find out. As they read in order to discuss the story with their peers and their teachers, they focus on making sense of stories and information. This internal dialogue is then shared in a collaborative exchange of ideas about the text.

When guiding students who are reading new text, teachers overlap what students already know and do in order to stretch the students' understanding. When we guide students' interpretations by using familiar ideas and strategies, they network connections, elaborating both the content and their strategies for understanding it. During this section of the lesson, the teacher looks for ways that readers can demonstrate their strengths, thus increasing their processing and understanding of text.

In keeping with good practice, experience with a new text or selection should include activities at three different points in the reading experience: before, during, and after reading (Walker, 1992a). Appropriate activities should be planned for each point in time. To refresh your memory in this regard, a sample lesson plan for new text is provided in Figure 6.1.

In this lesson framework, the teacher focused on constructing meaning both before and after reading, overlapping what the students already knew about different kinds of houses. The students had already listened to lots of stories, and the teacher used what they already could do to engage the students in reading the new story. Since the text was unfamiliar and provided a cognitive stretch, and since students were asked to construct an interpretation, adjustments made before, during, and after reading were needed to allow students to demonstrate their strengths—what they already knew and could do.

> In teaching new text, adjustments before, during, and after reading need to allow students to demonstrate their strengths.

FIGURE 6.1
Sample lesson plan

Book: *A House Is a House for Me* by Mary Ann Hoberman (1986).

Before Reading
Have children share different kinds of houses they have seen in their own life experiences. Make a semantic map (see Chapter Five) of their responses, such as the one shown:

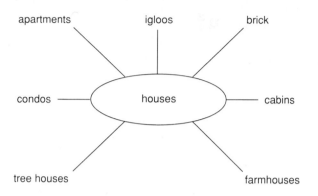

In constructing a semantic map, either on chart paper or on an overhead for the overhead projector, the children's background knowledge is activated and opportunities for organizing their collective ideas are provided.

During Reading
Using the shared reading activity (see Chapter Four) with the "read to, read with, you read" routine, first read the book to the class. On a second reading, invite them to join in the reading. Finally, have them read the book on their own or with a partner.

After Reading
Direct the children's attention back to the semantic map they constructed before reading. Using a different color marker, on the map record the houses they read about.

Now that the children have read the book and have an enlarged view of what may be considered a house, use another color marker to add other houses the children think of, but were not in the book. In this way they integrate new with old and "on their own" go beyond the text.

◆ ***Continuous Diagnostic Assessment:***   In continuous diagnostic assessment, assessment tools and procedures are used to examine specific reading behaviors. This may be as simple as a mini IRI on a story you are planning to use as new text.

By sampling students' reading behaviors, the teacher can anticipate problem areas.

By sampling students' reading behaviors in a particular text, both the students and the teacher can anticipate problem areas while checking the match between reader and text.

At other times, you may select a specific assessment tool (perhaps from your assessment tool catalog) to monitor reading behaviors—a think-aloud, perhaps, to assess comprehension. Or, use a retelling with familiar text read earlier in the lesson to determine how well the students understood the main idea and story sequence.

◆ ***Skill and Strategy Instruction (SAS):***   Walker (1992a) describes skill and strategy instruction as "a series of minilessons planned to develop and modify reading strategies" (p. 55). It is that time during instruction when the teacher, in effect, says, "Let me show you how to do what you need to do," explicitly telling about and modeling how a skill or strategy works. During these demonstrations, the teacher strives to concretely describe the reading process (print processing and meaning processing). Hence, skill and strategy instruction represents an opportune time to develop students' metacognitive abilities while targeting their specific weaknesses.

Because skill and strategy instruction is highly focused and intense, it needs to be short in duration (about 10 to 15 minutes). Following the teacher's demonstration, students need an opportunity to try out the new skill or strategy, preferably using texts at their independent level.

We advise using familiar text during SAS to teach "hard things" about written language. Remember this important learning principle: Connect the new with the known (Pearson & Johnson, 1978). When we use text that is familiar to children (the known), we can teach them new, and very often more difficult, skills related to written language. For example, vowel sounds are often hard to learn because they are a small, albeit necessary, bit of language. In a sea of unknown words, they are easily confused and often overlooked. But when examined in familiar text, they are easier to spot because the surrounding letters are well known and have meaning. So when examined in the context of familiar text, it's easier to make sense out of vowels and their vital role in print processing.

Similarly, developing an awareness of certain text structures (time order, cause-effect, etc.) that cue readers about the organization of information can more easily be grasped when students first understand the gist of a text; they are able then to focus on how it was organized. In other words, it's easier to "see" the subtler aspects of written language in familiar surroundings. Once readers see these aspects, they can get to know and use them. So, the teacher can use familiar text (actually, recycle it) to teach new skills in known print contexts.

Let us provide you with a concrete example. Mrs. Smith teaches second grade. Her students have read *The Tale of Peter Rabbit* by Beatrix Potter. She has written a brief summary of this familiar text to explore the notion of time order as signaled by specific words. She has developed a cloze procedure (see Chapter Four) as illustrated.

> Flopsy, Mopsy, and Cotton-tail were good bunnies. They went to gather
>
> blackberries. But naughty Peter ran to Mr. McGregor's garden and squeezed
>
> under the gate! _____ he ate lettuce and French beans; and
>
> _____ he ate radishes. And _____ , feeling sick, he
>
> went to look for parsley.

Notice that Mrs. Smith left out the words that signal time. She constructed this summary for that very purpose; it lends itself to the teaching of time order words.

Using an overhead, she has the children fill in the blanks with words they think will make sense. All answers are acceptable as long as they signal time and make sense. She points out how such words (e.g., first, next, then) cue readers to the passage of time in the story.

Later, Mrs. Smith will take another piece of familiar text and have her students practice using time order words while working with a partner. She reminds students that time order words convey passing time in a story and give clues about the organization of text.

Likewise, during skill and strategy instruction students need to be encouraged to articulate what they are doing as readers and how they know if a skill or strategy is working. They can also learn to self-evaluate their progress in a specific skill or strategy by using graphs, charts, or rating scales. The rating scale in Figure 6.2 provides one such example.

In brief, during SAS instruction students are "coached" into knowing how to do what they need to do to be healthy readers. Such instruction also provides the time a teacher needs to address specific weaknesses he has observed in children's reading behaviors (perhaps when reading familiar text) and to monitor their progress along these lines. There are additional spin-offs of SAS instruction, as well—the

FIGURE 6.2
Jenny's rating scale

As a reader, I . . .	a lot	some	a little	not at all
make guesses	|--|			
think of what I'm reading reminds me of	|--|			
check my thinking	|--|			
fix up problems	|--|			
share what I am thinking about the things I read	|--|			

development of children's metacognitive abilities and their competence at self-evaluation.

◆ *Personalized Reading and Writing (PRW):*   At the end of the instruction routine, the use of reading and writing must contribute to the quality of children's lives. In short, the energy they are asked to expend to learn literacy needs to be worth it *from their point of view.* So every lesson should "return to safe ground"—a comfortable place where readers and writers can enjoy what they are able to do. Usually this means using literacy for highly personal and functional reasons: reading a free-choice selection, personal journal writing, writing letters, designing games, reading old favorites, making scrapbooks, listening to a well-told story, or inviting others to share in some text they have found or produced.

> Every lesson should "return to safe ground," a comfortable place where readers and writers can enjoy what they are able to do.

From our point of view, it should be a rule that every reading experience ends in some personal and enjoyable way. This also makes good sense diagnostically, because a PRW time provides a window for observing what children like and what they can do on their own. In many respects, scheduling time for personal "play with print" points to the instructional direction we must eventually move.

As mentioned earlier, it is not our intent to make this instructional routine become a prescription for instruction. Rather, it is a means for organizing reading experiences for children. Activities in each phase will not necessarily occur every day, but will occur cyclically over time.

For example, in the classroom following warm up and a brief familiar text time, you may introduce a new text. You may spend an entire class period on prereading activities and then close with PRW time, focusing on literacy experiences perhaps connected with a previous selection. The next day, you may warm up, but perhaps skip familiar text time, moving on to the new text (during activities) and skill and strategy instruction, then closing with PRW. Another day, you may spend considerable time with familiar text, finish discussing the new text, conduct an assessment for the next day, and close with PRW.

In other words, the instructional routine functions in a cyclic way (not a linear one) as depicted in Figure 6.3. Hence the routine provides a structure, yet permits flexibility, lending itself to sustained work and connection-making. We do, however, strongly recommend that every reading experience begin with a warm up (ever so brief) and end enjoyably with personalized reading and writing time (even if just a quick return to an ongoing project).

To continue your understanding of the instructional routine, we have included four activities that will provide you with opportunities to develop your diagnostic teaching skills. In particular, you will

1. study how one teacher planned and conducted a multiday lesson for a small group of students, using the instructional routine.

FIGURE 6.3
The instructional
routine

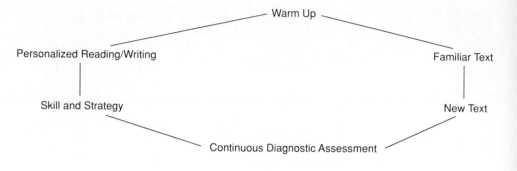

2. study and evaluate how one teacher planned and conducted a lesson for one student, using the instructional routine.
3. design a lesson, reflective of the instructional routine, for a small group of students based on the background data provided.
4. design and implement a lesson for an individual, using the instructional routine.

ACTIVITY 6.1	**Studying the Design of a Reading Lesson for a Group**

(*Note:* Read the first part on your own and do the second part with a cooperative group.)

What to Do First: Carefully read and study the instructional planning of Miss K. To help you understand her thinking processes, the lesson plan is prefaced by details about her class and her reading program. Note that actual implementation of the reading plan occurred over several consecutive days. Also note that the teacher has provided a rationale for each segment.

Background

The following plan was designed for a second-grade group of children. These children come from homes that engage children in many rich and unique experiences. Although these students are active thinkers when they discuss these experiences, they had extremely skill-focused instruction during first grade. Therefore, they are having difficulties constructing meaning from print, tending to sound out every word even when it does not follow the rules. The teacher wants to use a series of reading and writing experiences to engage students in the broader skills of predicting, confirming, and integrating. Her aim is to engage them in many meaning-centered activities. Using a literature-based reading program, she implements instructional techniques that model the reading process. In this particular lesson, she uses the following techniques: shared book, predict and confirm technique, word sorts, and the cloze procedure (see Chapter Four to review these techniques).

Instructional Plan

Key Literacy Concepts to be Developed:

1. Reading should make sense to the reader.
2. Readers are actively involved with the print. They make guesses and check their guesses with what they know and with the print. They make sense out of the printed message.

Objectives:

1. To develop students' abilities to make predictions about what they will read.
2. To develop students' abilities to confirm their predictions with printed cues and their own knowledge.
3. To enhance students' abilities to link what they read with their own lives.

◆ ***Warm Up:***   Read the directions and then create a hat out of newspaper. List characters the children could be while wearing their different hats. (Days one and two)

Why? To get started and to activate ideas for role-play.

◆ ***Familiar Text:***   Having read the book *Noisy Nora* by Rosemary Wells (1973) several times, students will explore the notion of cause-effect in a story. On chart paper, a few examples of cause-effect from daily life will be listed, for example, Why do you have a bandage on your finger? or Why are you wearing a sweater today? Then, an example from *Noisy Nora* will be provided. Students will offer others. Point out that the author used cause and effect as a way to organize the story *Noisy Nora*. (Day one)

On day two, have students find examples from other familiar texts of causes and effects. Have them record their findings on notebook paper.

Why? To develop awareness of a specific text structure.

◆ **New Text:** *Jillian Jiggs* by Phoebe Gilman (1985). This is a delightful, repetitive story about a little girl who loves to play games and to play "dressup." One minute she is a robot. The next she's a tree. But she hates to clean her room. Every time she begins, she thinks of something else to become and her play starts all over again.

Before Reading: Use a closed word sort with words from the story. Have students sort the words into two categories: action words (that tell what the children did) and character words (that tell what the children dress up as). (Day one)

Why? To develop familiarity with the main idea and vocabulary of the forthcoming story.

During Reading: Use the shared reading technique in a "read to, read with, you read" sequence to guide children through the text over a two-day period. On day one, read the story to the children, encouraging their comments about it. Then, read it to them again and ask them to join in the reading. Discuss the story further, relating it to their own experiences. On day two, read the story together as a group and then have students read the story with a partner.

Why? To focus on the meaning of the story, to model fluent reading, and to engage the children in fluent reading for meaning.

After Reading (Day one): Briefly discuss the story's main idea, connecting it to the children's daily lives. Then, with a partner, have the children complete the following cloze passage.

They dressed up as pirates, they dressed up as dr_____ .

They dressed up as tr_____ .

They dressed up as bad girls who never say pl_____ .

They dressed up as ch_____ , cooped up and caged.

They turned into monsters who hollered and r_____ .

Why? To read for meaning and to check guesses against the text.

After Reading (Day two): Engage the children in role-play, using the hats they developed in the warm-up activity. Have each child pantomime his/her character and have the other students guess, using the hat and gestures as clues. Guesses can be written on small slips of paper and then shared.

◆ **Continuous Diagnostic Assessment:**   As students read to their partners on day two, use the fluency rating scale (see Chapter Three, p. 57) to score fluency. Date and record the ratings on a class record sheet.

Why? To identify any problem areas for individual children and to keep a continuous record of their progress related to a concern in reading.

◆ **Skill and Strategy:**   Demonstrate the predict and confirm technique (see Chapter Four, p. 80) by using a piece of unfamiliar text at the children's independent level. Have the children participate, offering predictions and checking those predictions by using print and context cues. Do this each day over the two-day period.

Why? To develop children's print processing strategies of using what they think the text will say and then checking their guesses against the printed words.

◆ **Personalized Reading and Writing:**   Children write in their journals about their favorite activities.

Why? To have children use writing as a means of personal expression.

What to Do Next: Quickly review the instructional plan and answer the following questions.

(*Note:* Do this in your cooperative group.)

How did Miss K. focus on meaning?

How did the warm up set the stage for the new text activity?

How did the familiar text activity relate to the new text activity and/or work to develop strategies?

How did the new text activity utilize the students' strengths?

How did the plan develop both strengths and needs?

FOLLOW-UP DISCUSSION

Let's look again at this lesson. Did you notice how the warm-up and familiar text activities took only a short amount of time? These activities built a framework for thinking related to the new text, but they did not replace the new text. The familiar text activity used a well-known story to develop the notion of cause and effect, a critical aspect in understanding *Jillian Jiggs,* while the warm-up activity set the tone for the day-dreaming that the main character does. Both activities activated and worked on strategies related to the new text. The new text activities, especially after reading, focused on meaning using these strategies. To begin the new text activity, the teacher overlapped the new with the familiar by asking students to sort words according to action and character. By using the shared reading technique, the students heard and discussed the story, which created background knowledge that they could use later when they read the story on their own. These activities, because they were coherent, built toward a deeper understanding of the story. The skill and strategy instruction focused on the process of word identification (predict and confirm) within a meaningful written context of an easy-to-read text. Although this was a shift, it provided practice in a strategy that the students needed, thus extending their strategy development. The continuous diagnostic assessment monitored fluency development, while personalized reading and writing helped students make choices related to their own literacy. The entire lesson provided a framework for advancing the students' reading development.

Of course, a routine does not instruction make. It provides a framework for action, but it does not provide the activities that teachers and learners do together. Just as the teacher's interpretation of data brings meaning to diagnosis, her skillful lesson planning brings meaning to an instructional routine. Since "any form of learning can deal with the intellectually trivial as well as the intellectually significant" (Eisner & Vallance, 1974, p. 14), what is called for is the thoughtful orchestration of content (what is to be learned) and process (how it is learned). As Eliot Eisner (1990) points out, "No matter how well something is taught, if it is not worth teaching, it is not worth teaching well" (p. 524). In this respect, the teacher must be a "designer" of reading experiences who makes judgments about what, as well as how, she will engage children in reading endeavors.

Given the inclusion of the basic elements of lesson planning (purpose, objectives, procedure, materials, and evaluation), there are at least two design considerations in lesson planning: coherence and balance.

Coherence means that the reading activities we use throughout the instructional routine (warm up, familiar text, new text, CDA, SAS, and PRW) are connected in some way, that is, they interrelate or "hang together" along some common thread. For instance, all of the reading activities done throughout the instructional routine may coalesce on a common theme or topic, such as, friendship, survival, pollution, or dinosaurs.

To cohere, the reading activities children do need to be internally *consistent* as well, in that each activity must contribute to the accomplishment of the overarching goals of the lesson. For example, one major goal of reading instruction is to assist children in realizing that reading is a meaning-making process. The set of activities we engage children in, then, should consistently support that goal.

Coherence also implies that reading activities are *congruent*, fitting together harmoniously. When activities cohere, they weave a net of connections that support concept development and learning. One activity builds on the next, consistently cueing students about content and the reading process. As a result, the experience becomes meaningful, creating a sense of satisfaction and enjoyment.

Another important consideration in lesson design is **balance.** Somewhat like Goldilocks, for whom things needed to feel "just right," lessons "feel right" when they balance the familiar and the new, strategy and skill instruction, forms of written language and its functions, the personal and the academic, student-led activities and teacher-led efforts. Balance as a design factor in lesson planning develops a sense of stability and equilibrium in learning, which also contributes to enjoyment. Furthermore, being alert to balance in reading activities ensures that readers' strengths, as well as their needs, are addressed—not to mention their overall control of the reading process.

How do successful teachers achieve coherence and balance in the reading experiences they offer children? Very carefully! They plan utilizing two resources: (1) their knowledge base, to decide on content and purposes (concepts and objectives) and to rationalize their choices, and (2) their personal reflections on past instruction to feed future plans. As a result, successful teachers design coherent and balanced reading lessons that match students' strengths and needs while remaining open to "teachable moments."

Coherence means that activities are connected to one another, are consistently focused on learner goals, and are congruent or fit together.

Balance develops a sense of stability and equilibrium in learning.

| **ACTIVITY 6.2** | **Judging the Design of a Reading Lesson** |

(*Note:* Do the first part of the activity on your own and the second part with a partner.)

What to Do First: Carefully read and study the instructional planning of Mr. R. To help you understand his thinking processes, the lesson plan is prefaced by details about Ricardo, one of his students. Note that Mr. R has provided a rationale for each activity segment.

Background

Ricardo is a reserved fifth-grade boy who decodes words readily. He has had a lot of experiences in his home and in the Mexican-American community where he lives. In the first and second grades, Ricardo was considered a star student who worked diligently on his worksheets. Proud of his oral reading ability, he read words without thinking about their meaning. During third and fourth grades, however, reading became more difficult. He didn't understand what he was reading, nor did he know how to change his reading behavior. He could still sound out most of the words, but somehow reading all the words correctly did not help him get the questions right. When he read orally, he phrased improperly, not stopping at periods. Ricardo was reading the words in the text without thinking about what he was reading or what he knew related to what he was reading. He seldom used his vast knowledge when he read. Since fourth grade, he began to think of himself as a failure and withdrew more and more from classroom experiences that involved literacy.

Instructional Plan

Key Literacy Concepts to be Developed:

1. Oral reading should sound the way we talk and think.
2. Reading means using what you know to interpret what you are reading.

Objectives:

1. To develop more fluency in reading
2. To engage the student in using background knowledge to interpret text
3. To improve reading comprehension and self-questioning

◆ **Warm Up:**   Read personal writing and my response from previous lesson. (After the last session, I wrote a personal note to Ricardo about his basketball experiences.)
     Why? To establish the literacy context by relating to a previous lesson.

◆ **Familiar Text:**   Reread *Too Much Noise* by Ann McGovern (1967). I will read a page, modeling phrasing, and then Ricardo will read the next page.
     Why? To connect the strategy of reading in phrases to form thoughts, I will use this short story because it has rhyme, repetition of familiar phrases, and predictable passages about animals. Ricardo knows the predictable story about familiar farm animals and the repetitive story line; therefore, he can focus on fluent reading in thought units.

◆ **New Text:**   After trying out several novels, Ricardo chose *The Boy Who Owned the School* by Gary Paulsen (1991). This is an easy-to-read and funny chapter book about a boy whose life goal is to go about school unnoticed. Yet, as he falls in love, he finds himself the center of attention.
     Why? This novel fits Ricardo's interests (self-chosen) and his reading level (oral reading 1/40, fluency average, and comprehension 70%; silent reading comprehension 70%—but responses sketchy). Ricardo readily identifies with the main character.

Before Reading: Explain the ReQuest technique (see Chapter Five, p. 102) where the student and the teacher take turns asking and answering questions. Then read the title of the book and ask Ricardo prediction questions. Have Ricardo read the first paragraph silently. When he is finished, have him ask questions about the main character (in this case, Jacob).

During Reading: For the next four paragraphs, take turns asking the questions. Then, have Ricardo finish reading the chapter on his own.

After Reading: Begin a character map of Jacob. (See Figure 6.4. Also see semantic mapping in Chapter Five, p. 108.) Put descriptive words on the map and write the chapter number that the idea came from. After reading each chapter, add to the semantic map.

Why? The ReQuest technique develops active reading—Ricardo will read to find questions to stump the teacher. Because this is a chapter book, a character map can be used after each chapter to follow how the character develops throughout the book. Tomorrow the "before reading" activity will start with a review of the character map and a prediction.

◆ **Continuous Diagnostic Assessment:** Have Ricardo read the first paragraph of the next chapter silently. Ask Ricardo five questions about this section. Identify any word-meaning problems.

Why? This will help me match this text with Ricardo's reading performance and will identify what he knows about the chapter, as well as any problem areas for this next lesson.

◆ **Skill and Strategy:** Demonstrate the self-directed questioning technique (see Chapter Five, p. 104) using "What Do You Come For?" from *More Scary Stories to Tell in the Dark* by Alvin Schwartz (1984). I will model predicting and revising "bets," as well as thinking aloud about the clues I use, saying "I bet . . . because the text says . . . I know that . . ." When I am wrong, I will say, "Oops, I made a mistake."

As Ricardo reads and thinks aloud about the second short story, I will use the source-of-information chart (Figure 6.5) and give him a point for each statement (prediction or explanation) that reflects his use of background knowledge or of the text. When Ricardo's statements reflect the integration of background knowledge and the text, he will receive a point in both columns of the chart.

Why? Ricardo is a very passive reader who seldom uses his own knowledge while reading, either orally or silently. This interferes with his comprehension and fluency. By encouraging Ricardo to use what he knows when making predictions, Ricardo will elaborate comprehension and, I hope, increase fluency. I will use ghost stories not only because of Ricardo's familiarity with the story structure, but also because the ambiguity of these stories will allow him to make and revise predictions. The short length also allows me to model the whole story during one sitting.

The charting of the sources of information Ricardo uses will help him understand how to use both background knowledge and text together. It will also help him see that he mostly uses the text without thinking about what he knows. He will begin to think about what he already knows as we chart his thinking.

◆ **Personalized Reading and Writing:** At the end of the session, Ricardo chose to read a favorite story during sustained silent reading. I will end the day writing in his journal. After the last session, he chose to write about his basketball

FIGURE 6.4
Character map

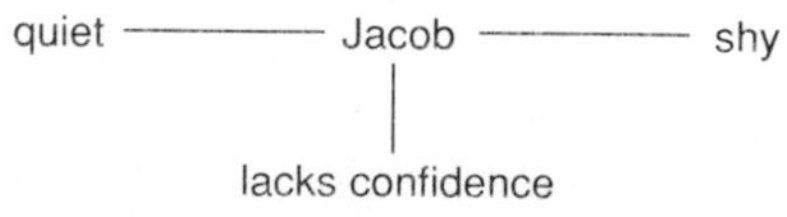

quiet ———— Jacob ———— shy
|
lacks confidence

Sources of Information

I Used What I Know

||

I Used the Text

‖‖‖ ‖‖

game. I wrote a personal note inquiring about how he thought the next game would go. I hope he will continue to write about his interests.

Why? During this time Ricardo will make choices about his reading and writing, allowing him to define his own reasons for engaging in literacy activities. As he does this, he will not fail, but instead will begin to think of himself as a reader and a writer.

What to Do Next: Now you will have an opportunity to judge, using the criteria of coherence and balance, the design of Mr. R's lesson. Remember that a coherent lesson is one that is connected, internally consistent, and congruent. A balanced lesson includes comparable portions of the personal and the academic as well as the known and the new.

To facilitate your analysis, we have provided a Lesson Design Checklist. The checklist is divided into two parts: one lists indicators of coherence, the other indicators of balance. In each part, you respond to the indicators by answering Yes (Y), Somewhat (S), or No (N).

A "Yes" is worth 2 points, a "Somewhat" worth 1 point, and a "No" receives a 0. The sum of the points earned compared to the total possible points indicates the extent of coherence and balance in the lesson (high, medium, or low). Using this procedure, you can judge the overall design of Mr. R's lesson, basing your evaluation on the ratings of coherence and balance.

Lesson Design Checklist

Part 1

Indicator	Coherence		
	Y	S	N
1. The warm up connects home, school, and lesson.			
2. The familiar text activity is congruent with either the targeted strategy or the new text.			
3. The new text activity reinforces reading as a meaning-making activity.			
4. SAS is consistent with identified concerns.			
5. CDA monitors performance in the new text or progress in skills and strategies.			
6. PRW enhances reading and writing for individual purposes.			

Yes = 2; Somewhat = 1; No = 0
Total Score = /12

Part 2

Indicator	Balance		
	Y	S	N
1. Strengths and weaknesses are addressed.			
2. Challenging and easy activities are included.			
3. Familiar and new texts are used.			
4. Skills and strategies are developed.			
5. Personal and academic activities are included.			
6. Student-led and teacher-led activities are included.			

Yes = 2; Somewhat = 1; No = 0
Total Score = /12

Rating
The coherence is   _____ high (9–12 points)
                      _____ medium (5–8 points)
                      _____ low (below 5 points)

Rating
The balance is   _____ high (9–12 points)
                      _____ medium (5–8 points)

                      _____ low (below 5 points)

Overall, the design
of this lesson is
                      _____ Superior or High (18–24 points)
                      _____ Good or Medium (10–17 points)
                      _____ Low (below 10 points)

FOLLOW-UP DISCUSSION

How did you rate this instructional plan overall? We gave it a high rating. Its primary strength is the balanced development of strategies and skills for direct application in familiar and new texts. For the most part, it provided Ricardo with a coherent and balanced reading experience and most likely an enjoyable one.

Using the Lesson Design Checklist, you can judge the overall design of your own lessons, basing your evaluations on the ratings of coherence and balance. We think that the checklist can become a useful resource for you in your professional work. It is a quick means of analyzing your own instructional planning, revealing the design quality of the reading experiences into which you invite children.

Undoubtedly, most of the lessons you plan will fall into the medium range, simply because you will not always be at your peak performance; no one is. Some of your lessons, however, will be superior, with high coherence and balance. When they are you will know it immediately, because they will be very satisfying teaching experiences for you and memorable learning experiences for children.

As professionals, we need to strive for excellence in designing reading experiences for children. When such experiences are coherent and balanced, they are worth doing. By designing such experiences, we truly integrate literacy into the lives of children in ways that empower them.

ACTIVITY 6.3   ## Designing a Reading Experience for a Group

(*Note:* Do this activity in a cooperative group of 6 to 8. A subgroup (3 or 4) needs to work together to design the lesson. During the second part of the activity ("What to do next"), the subgroups will exchange plans to evaluate them. Then the entire group looks at the plans together.)

What to Do First: Now, using the instructional routine as a planning guide, it's your turn to design a reading experience. It is a "run up" to the diagnostic teaching of real students.

We want you to pretend that you are the teacher of a small (and wonderful) group of children. We have provided background information about this group—where they are instructionally and where they need to be going. We have also provided you with a selection to use as new text for this group, or you may decide to use a selection of your own choice. It is your task to design a reading experience for them based on the selection. Before you begin, just a few reminders: (1) Remember that your lesson can span a couple of days, if necessary. (2) Be sure to include rationales for the activities you select in each phase of the instructional routine. (3) Strive to link the activities with the concepts you are assisting children in coming to know.

To facilitate your efforts, a lesson plan format is provided for you. We also encourage you to evaluate your lesson design using the Lesson Design Checklist. Finally, when all is said and done, consider sharing and discussing your design with a friend.

Background Information about the Group

This is a group of six boisterous and humorous fourth graders (4 boys; 2 girls) who are reading below grade level. As a whole, the group tends to "gloss over" the text, not reading for meaning nor with fluency. They tend to be word callers, anxious to get the reading over with and get on to something more interesting.

They all have highly developed graphophonemic skills, having experienced exclusively skill-based instruction where phonics were emphasized. Thus these students can decode content vocabulary words, but rarely are able to use these meaningfully to gain information in continuous text sequences.

All of these children dislike reading and will tell you so. They think it is boring, and would never choose to do it as a leisure activity. In brief, they approach reading with extreme reluctance, avoiding it by being noisy, silly, and sometimes sassy.

Instructional Plan

Using the story "Don't Pick That Scab" by Marcy Lidtke (1991) (found on page 137), develop your lesson using the instructional routine format.

Instructional Routine	Plan	Why?
Warm up		
Familiar text		
New text Before		
During		
After		
Continuous diagnostic assessment		
Personalized reading and writing		

What to Do Next: Exchange lesson plans with a subgroup of your cooperative group. Take out the Lesson Design Checklist and evaluate the lesson plan.

What to Do Last: Now, take a moment to compare the plans developed in your cooperative group with the plan of another student, given in Figure 6.6. First, you will need to evaluate the student's plan using the Lesson Design Checklist. Take note of how your plans differ with his plan, but also how much you agree with him. Both the plans you generated and this student's plan represent the planning of beginning teachers. In this respect, we need to be mindful that effective planning takes experience and practice.

FIGURE 6.6
Sample lesson plan

Instructional Routine	Plan	Why?
Warm up	On a diagram of the heart, students will map the route of blood through the heart.	To activate background knowledge and set tone for reading. To introduce the heart and its function.
Familiar text	Read ''Band-Aids'' by Shel Silverstein.	To teach a skill from the course of study, e.g., capitalization.
New text		
Before	Discuss worst scabs. Draw a picture of the incident that caused it and write a brief paragraph describing it.	To set purpose for reading. To elicit interest.
During	Begin with ReQuest for first 3 paragraphs. Then finish reading silently, individually.	To involve in text.
After	Have students graphically depict the ''life cycle'' of a scab.	To integrate new information with background. To enhance comprehension.
Continuous diagnostic assessment	Point out the value of drawing pictures after reading. Tell the students this is one way to remember what was read. Practice with a selection from the science text.	Provide a concrete strategy for students to use on their own as an aid to comprehension. To transfer a strategy to a content area text.
Personalized reading and writing	Continue the before-reading writing activity by having students extend, revise, and edit paragraphs.	Provide a purpose for writing. Relax and reflect about own experiences in relation to the text.

FOLLOW-UP DISCUSSION

How did your comparison and evaluation go? We rated the plan in the medium range. One weakness we noted was that the continuous diagnostic assessment activity did not monitor performance, but rather introduced an entirely new skill, making the lesson less coherent and balanced. What kind of continuous assessment did you suggest? One suggestion might be to construct a cloze assessment from a science textbook to lead into a new text the following day. Then you could ascertain if the text was appropriate for the students' reading performance. If it was, you could use the suggested activities in a new lesson plan.

Also, did you notice how the rationales included ideas relating the planning activity to the theory of reading? This showed that the teacher was thinking about how the plan promoted active reading; however, the rationales did not reflect the strengths and needs of this group of students.

As you begin teaching, it is not easy to include all the complex aspects of instruction; nevertheless, coherence and balance in your instructional plans are important goals. When buttressed by rationales that address students' strengths and needs, such planning supports children's reading development and growth.

Hypothetical instructional plans are challenging to write and discuss, but they do not replace planning lessons and implementing them with real children. Therefore, we end this chapter with a practical application exercise.

Don't Pick That Scab*

A scab on your knee is yukky-looking. And it may itch a little. There's always a temptation to pick it off. **Don't do that.**

So you fell off your bike. Or tripped on a broken sidewalk. Or scraped your knee climbing up a tree. Lots of everyday things like that will break your skin so that blood oozes out.

The blood that your heart is pumping all the time flows through your body in special tubes. Close to the heart the tubes are large, and are called arteries and veins. But farther away, the tubes get smaller and smaller. Just under your skin are some of the tiniest tubes of all. They are called capillaries.

A cut bleeds because blood leaks out of the damaged capillaries. A little bleeding is good. It helps clean out any dirt. You can help, too, by washing the wound with running water, and soap if it's available. Do that, even if it hurts a little. Then the job is to stop the bleeding. You can help by putting on an adhesive bandage or by lightly pressing a clean tissue over the cut.

But the main job of stopping leaks is something your body does all by itself. Your blood takes on the first part of the job. Right at the leak the blood changes into a very thick jelly that gradually hardens to plug up the capillaries. And that's what a scab is—a plug that seals off the capillaries.

Once a scab has formed, your body can start its repair job. There are special white cells, always carried in your blood, that work as a clean-up crew to get rid of germs and pieces of dirt too tiny to see. They also become part of the scab.

Then the cells of your skin get in the act. They grow new cells that begin to form new skin right underneath the scab. Most of the other parts of your body can't be replaced if they are lost. But your skin is special in being able to make new skin—even with the same little lines and creases that were there before.

After a few days, the new skin will begin to build new capillaries, and the scabby place may get especially itchy. Peeking under a scab won't help. It is likely to start the bleeding again so that everything has to start over.

About a week later, the scab will just fall off or soak off in the bathtub. In place of the scab will be your new skin, maybe lighter in color at first, but good as new.

When the scab has gone—all by itself—and you can see that new skin, give yourself a gold star for doing your part and leaving the scab alone.

*Used by permission of Highlights for Children, Inc. Columbus, OH. Copyright © 1991.

ACTIVITY 6.4   **Using the Instructional Routine**

(*Note:* Try this activity on your own.)

What to Do: For this activity, you will need a student with whom you will conduct one or two tutorial sessions. Once you find a willing volunteer, you need to plan a reading experience for him or her, just as you developed a full-fledged one for your pretend group in the previous activity. Consider audiotaping the tutorial sessions, so you can review and analyze your own teaching. After the experience, take some time to "debrief" with a friend.

Summary

In this chapter you became acquainted with an instructional routine that supports diagnostic teaching. This routine includes six activities: a warm up, familiar text time, new text experiences, skill and strategy lessons, continuous diagnostic assessment, and personalized reading and writing opportunities. Not intended as a prescription, the routine provides a framework for lesson design and implementation.

You also examined two elements of lesson design—coherence and balance. When these elements are present, even to a moderate degree, in diagnostic reading instruction, children tend to experience reading in ways that are satisfying and enjoyable.

Finally, you became involved in several activities which asked you to evaluate and develop instructional plans, utilizing the instructional routine and incorporating the elements of design. These experiences provided you with some hands-on diagnostic teaching. In the next chapter, you will continue to develop your diagnostic teaching skills, learning how to reflect on and evaluate your own teaching.

Further Reading

Baskwill, J. (1989). *The whole language sourcebook*. Toronto, Canada: Scholastic. Packed with practical ideas and strategies, this text provides many examples of warm-up activities, things to do with familiar texts, ways to introduce new texts, and extension activities.

Clay, M. M. (1985). *The early detection of reading difficulties: A diagnostic survey with recovery procedures* (3rd ed.). Portsmouth, NH: Heinemann. This book elaborates a structured format for diagnostic teaching of children at risk in first grade. The format includes: Reading of familiar stories (familiar text activity); taking a running record (continuous diagnostic assessment), working with letters, writing a message or story, and reading a new book (reading new text).

Johnson, T., & Louis, D. (1987). *Literacy through literature*. Portsmouth, NH: Heinemann. Provides a wide range of ways to use teaching techniques, such as the cloze procedure, with children's literature. Also includes a number of creative variations of commonly used procedures.

Walker, B. J. (1992). *Diagnostic teaching of reading: Techniques for instruction and assessment* (2nd ed.). New York: Merrill/Macmillan. This book offers a structured format for diagnostic teaching using four elements: Guided contextual reading (new text); skill and strategy instruction, continuous diagnostic assessment, and personalized reading and writing. It elaborates these lesson elements and provides rationales for each in diagnostic teaching.

PART THREE

Applying the Process and Procedures of Reading Diagnosis

In Part Three we focus on the convergence of the diagnostic process, procedures, and instructional techniques and their application to problem situations involving readers and writers. Through case studies, which describe the reading behaviors of small groups of children or provide accounts of an individual's reading, we introduce you to problem readers and ask you to make decisions about their reading performances and about appropriate instructional techniques that you might use to teach these students.

Chapter Seven, in particular, provides you with many opportunities to practice observing, analyzing, interpreting, translating, and reflecting in reference to individual problem readers as well as problem readers within a group. In short, you will use the diagnostic process to make decisions about children's reading strengths and instructional needs. Within the framework of the activities you will do, you will encounter different mechanisms that facilitate the application of diagnosis to teaching. For example, you will learn how to employ the features matrix you used in Chapter Two as a means of analyzing the reading strengths and needs of a reading group. These analytic devices should prove valuable in your later educational work.

Chapter Eight briefly elaborates the concept of reflecting in teaching, involving you in a closer examination of the dynamics of this mental activity. The activities you will do invite you into the minds of novice teachers as they rethink the decisions they have made and the teaching they have done.

Thus, Part Three requires that you "put it all together," engaging you in all facets of the decision making central to diagnostic teaching. This is done in a way that simulates the reading behaviors of real readers and writers with real instructional problems, providing you with insights about the application of diagnosis in your own teaching.

CHAPTER SEVEN

◆

Reading Diagnosis at Work

◆————————————◆

... errors are the portals of discovery
—James Joyce

In the preceding chapters you participated in activities that developed your understanding of different aspects of reading diagnosis. You examined its foundations, experienced its process, tried its procedures, and used instructional techniques that develop healthy reader strategies.

However, by now you may be feeling that you need "another think," as our childhood friend Winnie-the-Pooh was so often wont to do. So, in this chapter, we provide you with "another think" about reading diagnosis. You will have an opportunity to integrate the process and procedures of diagnosis with teaching techniques, applying your knowledge to actual classroom situations and individual case studies.

Reading diagnosis indicates an entry point for instruction and informs the ongoing course of instruction.

In general, reading diagnosis becomes a part of reading instruction in two basic ways. One, diagnosis is used to indicate an entry point for instruction, for example, what level of reading material to use, what selections match readers' interests, and what initial instructional techniques seem most appropriate. Two, diagnosis is used to inform the ongoing course of reading instruction, revealing student progress as well as needs. You may not be as aware of diagnosis in this role, since it tends to be embedded in almost imperceptible moments of instruction. For example, a teacher may notice that a student is reluctant to make predictions. She observes this behavior more closely in subsequent reading experiences, assessing the frequency and quality of predictions. She interprets her findings and makes a judgment about the acceptability of the behavior. Her evaluation is then translated into teaching actions: she adapts her teaching to meet the needs of the learner within the instructional process. All this can happen very, very quickly in the ebb and flow of instruction.

To diagnose reading behaviors and to teach at the same time, adjusting your instruction as you go, is no easy trick! Even for veteran teachers, this kind of "diagnosing-on-your-feet" while teaching is a challenge. Nevertheless, if diagnosis is to become a genuine part of instruction, it must be deliberately worked into the fabric of one's teaching. Of course, as you may already realize, to develop this skill demands *practice*.

Using diagnosis as an entry point for instruction and as a means of gathering information during instruction involves teachers in certain decision-making activities. For example, they need to decide what assessment tools to use and when, how to analyze what they see and what the findings mean, and finally, what teaching techniques to employ to address students' specific needs.

141

On the following pages, we briefly describe these decision-making activities, along with questions that often accompany them. We present them here to give you an overview of the process you will be practicing in the forthcoming activities. As you will note, the different decision-making "points" reflect different phases of the diagnosis cycle previously discussed in Chapter Two. These decision points represent those times before and during instruction when the teacher's understanding of the diagnostic process and its practice converge to inform and support his instruction. Examine each decision-making point carefully, noting in particular the questions associated with each. As a set, these questions provide a framework for putting diagnosis to work in instruction.

Observation

DECISION POINT:
Selecting Appropriate Informal Assessment Tools

Whether initiating an instructional sequence or in the midst of one, the teacher needs to decide on what assessment tools to use to gather information. Three questions guide tool selection:

1. How can I systematically observe what I need to see?
2. What assessment tool(s) will easily provide the most data?
3. Do the tools provide multiple points of view?

Analysis

DECISION POINT:
Using Analytic Procedures/Summarizing Diagnostic Data

Remember our brief discussion about analysis in Chapter Two? *Analysis* is a word that is used frequently, but seems difficult to put into action. Since it means "taking things apart," this is what we want the procedures we use to do—to "take apart" readers' behaviors so we can have a closer look. You need to select procedures that will allow you to do this efficiently and effectively with the data you gather. After all, instructionally you have places to go and things to do. So, be choosy!

Close on the heels of your analyzing is putting it all back together again. You need to organize your findings into meaningful "bits." We highly recommend generating summary statements to accomplish this goal. Summary statements allow you to condense information into a more manageable form, facilitating the interpreting you must do next. Some questions you may find helpful during the analysis phase of diagnosis are

1. Which analytic procedure(s) will likely yield the most from this information?
2. What findings seem to "jump out at me?"
3. How can I state the big findings in a few words? How can I summarize the information into a few key ideas?

Interpretation

DECISION POINT:
Noting Patterns of Reading Behavior

This phase requires multiple readings of the findings to ascertain patterns of strength and need in the reader's behaviors. Some questions to ask yourself are

1. What reading behaviors (predicting, confirming, integrating) stand out as strengths? as stumbling blocks?
2. How does the reader process print, that is, how are the language systems used?
3. How does the reader process meaning, that is, how is meaning constructed?
4. How appropriate are the reader's behaviors developmentally?
5. How much control of the reading process does the reader demonstrate?

Translation ◯

DECISION POINT:
Choosing Instructional Techniques and Reader Strategies That Enhance Strengths and Target Needs

As we have said before, diagnostic activity is only worth doing if it leads to instructional adjustments and change; it is a means to an end, not the end. To facilitate the use of diagnosis, the following questions may be used to guide this phase of decision making:

1. What teaching techniques will support strengths and will target needs?
2. What strategies does the reader need to know and do?
3. How do these strategies impact the reader's behaviors?

By quickly and deliberately using these decision-making activities both at the onset of instruction and in the flow of it, the teacher is essentially making an effort to link what she sees (through observation, analysis, and interpretation) with what she does (translation into instruction). In addition, she periodically "distances" herself from these decision-making activities to reflect about her decisions and to construct rationales for them. In this way she systematically and thoughtfully approaches and implements the diagnostic teaching of reading.

Now, to acquaint you with diagnosis at work in these ways, we will involve you in two major activities. These activities provide that oft-mentioned (and needed) practice in using reading diagnosis to make instructional decisions for small groups and for individuals. We think it is particularly important to include diagnostic decision making with groups, because so much of classroom life is concerned with small-group instruction.

Specifically you will work through six activities, three of which involve you in diagnostic decision making with respect to an individual (Activities 7.2, 7.3, and 7.5) and three of which ask you to make diagnostic decisions for a small group (Activities 7.1, 7.4, and 7.6). In each set of activities you will need to

♦ *select* assessment tools to conduct observations;
♦ *analyze* data and generate written summary statements;
♦ *interpret* findings in the form of written summaries, noting patterns of reading behavior;
♦ *translate* your interpretations into practice by choosing instructional techniques that bolster readers' strengths and target their needs.

To assist you in developing these skills, we have focused on one or two in each activity. For example, Activities 7.1 and 7.2 involve you in selecting assessment tools. But keep in mind that, although you are practicing the skills of diagnosis almost one-by-one, they occur dynamically and in concert in actual teaching practice.

Furthermore, because these activities simulate actual classroom diagnostic practices, they will require considerable time and commitment on your part. Consequently, allow yourself ample time to work through the activities, consciously applying what you have learned in previous chapters to the cases.

ACTIVITY 7.1	**What-When-Why: Selecting Assessment Tools for a Small Group**

(*Note:* You may want to do this activity with a partner. You may also find the catalog in Chapter Two helpful.)

What to Do: In this activity you will select assessment tools that you think will aid you in making instructional decisions for a small group. Carefully read the following case. Then, using the worksheet that follows the case study, indicate what assessment tools you will use, when, and why.

Case Study:
Observing the Reading Behaviors of First Graders in an Urban Elementary School

It is August and you have been hired as a first-grade teacher at Sunview Elementary School in a large metropolitan area. The school serves a kindergarten through third-grade population of 600 children. Your class of twenty-five children includes five bilingual Spanish-speaking children, ten children identified as "at-risk" by the previous kindergarten teacher, and two children who appear exceptionally advanced. Many of the children reside in single-parent homes. Over half have spent early childhood in poverty. During the kindergarten year, no formal testing was conducted; the primary assessment procedure was a checklist of discrete reading skills, for example, "The child is able to recognize upper and lower case letters of the alphabet." The school uses a traditional basal approach to reading instruction; however, the principal is supportive of alternatives to basal instruction, as long as the adopted curriculum is covered.

What to Do Next: Now use the worksheet to indicate what assessment tools you would use to learn more about the literacy development of your class. Think about and decide on a timetable for your diagnostic activities. Provide a rationale for what you are doing.

Assessment Tool Selection Worksheet (Group)

Assessment Tool	*Time Frame*	*Rationale*

FOLLOW-UP DISCUSSION

What did you decide to do for your first graders at Sunview Elementary? Compare your decisions with those of Mary and Andy, prospective elementary teachers.

Like Mary and Andy, you may have decided to use some kind of print orientation assessment and to obtain a writing sample. Together these would provide information for interpreting the children's development of print awareness and knowledge. In particular, you could assess children's concepts in the following areas:

◆ writing conventions (book handling, left-to-right and top-to-bottom orientation);
◆ the relationship between picture and print;
◆ sense of word and letter; and
◆ stage of spelling development.

You may have also included one or two other assessments, such as an interest inventory to determine the potential reading interests and preferences of your class. Such information would assist your instructional decision making related to literature choices for shared reading and "read to" sessions.

Considering it is the beginning of the school year, you may have decided to conduct the assessments during the first week of school. Working with small groups of three to five children, the writing samples could easily be obtained in daily ten-minute blocks of time devoted to this purpose. The print orientation assessment would need to be scheduled at times when you could work with individual children for about 5 to 7 minutes, perhaps during language arts or reading time.

Undoubtedly the timetable you devised will vary from that of someone else, but it should reflect small blocks of time devoted to the assessment of small groups and individual students.

Having "wet your feet" so to speak, in the next activity you will encounter a slightly more complex situation. It is a case study of a youngster whose mother is very concerned about his reading progress.

FIGURE 7.1
Mary's and Andy's assessment tool selection

Assessment Tool	Time Frame	Rationale
Print orientation assessment	Weeks 1 and 2 (during Free Choice)	To determine children's basic concepts about print, e.g., knowledge that print is what is read
Writing sample	Weeks 1 and 2 (whole group)	To determine approximate spelling stage of development
		To assess writing fluency and sense of audience
Interest inventory	Week 1 (whole group)	To determine common group interests and specific individual tastes

ACTIVITY 7.2

What-When-Why: Selecting Assessment Tools for an Individual

(*Note:* You may want to do this activity with a partner. Again, the tool catalog in Chapter Two may be useful.)

What to Do: As in the previous activity, carefully read the following case. Then decide what assessment tools you will use, when, and why.

Case Study: Observing the Reading Behaviors of a Third Grader

Kamal is in the third grade of a suburban elementary school. As reported by his teacher, Kamal has a very positive attitude about school and gets along well with others: "Students like him and he likes them." However, Kamal's teacher is concerned that he reads below grade level and seems to lack focus or concentration during reading and reading-related activities. His teacher feels that reading has become a stumbling block for Kamal, especially in content areas like social studies and science. She wants to know why he reads so poorly and what she can do about it.

Kamal's mother refers to him as "a poor reader" who does not enjoy reading. She is worried that he may get too far behind and lose interest in school. She has noticed that he sounds out words slowly and has difficulty with vowel sounds. She says: "Sometimes, he likes to guess, instead of taking his time to sound out a word." Over the last few months, Kamal's mother has observed some improvement in his reading: "He reads with better expression and seems to understand more of what he is reading." However, without additional help, she does not feel he can progress satisfactorily.

What to Do Next: Use the worksheet to indicate what assessment tools you would use to learn more about Kamal's reading behaviors. Think about and decide on a timetable for your diagnostic activities. Provide reasons why you choose to do what you will do.

Assessment Tool Selection Worksheet (Individual)

Assessment Tool	Timetable	Rationale

FOLLOW-UP DISCUSSION

Considering our third grader, Kamal, what did you decide to do? Again, compare your ideas to those of another student, Jane, provided in Figure 7.2.

As Jane has indicated, a reading interview would be very helpful. It may reveal Kamal's perceptions of the reading process, indicating his beliefs about what an effective reader does to achieve success. Furthermore, an interest inventory would aid in pinpointing Kamal's interests and preferences, information needed to stimulate Kamal's recreational reading.

To gain an overall sense of Kamal's reading behaviors, an informal reading inventory seems most efficient. Using this tool, it is possible to determine Kamal's approximate reading level, as well as his print and meaning processing. Conducting a miscue analysis of the oral reading portion, it is possible to ascertain how Kamal is using his language systems (semantic, syntactic, and graphophonemic) to process print; this analysis would also point toward strengths and weaknesses in Kamal's graphophonemic system.

On the silent reading portion of the inventory, retellings could be requested. These could be analyzed to assess what contributes to Kamal's meaning processing. To what extent does he use existing schemata? Text-based information? Does he integrate both to infer meaning? What about his understanding of key vocabulary?

If retellings prove too challenging for Kamal, the comprehension questions that accompany passages in most IRIs could be used. These could then be analyzed as to type, indicating Kamal's ability to construct meaning with text at literal, interpretive, and applied levels.

You may have selected a few other tools to use with Kamal, for example, a writing sample or the Names Test. Those tools previously cited, however, seem essential for determining how Kamal thinks about and with print. Your timetable for Kamal may have included some before- or after-school sessions. Or, you may have asked the reading resource person to assist you in your assessment of Kamal's reading behaviors.

As a result of this activity, you may have a clearer sense as to why it is important to be familiar with a variety of assessment tools and procedures. Selecting the right tool at the right time saves time and facilitates instructional decision making.

In the next two activities, you will go beyond the selection of assessment tools to the analysis and interpretation of data. Both require substantial mental effort, beginning with taking things apart and ending with putting them all back together into an interpretation that makes sense based on the evidence. First we will analyze and interpret the reading behaviors of an individual, our student Kamal; then we will turn our attention to those of a small group of third graders—a somewhat greater analytic challenge.

FIGURE 7.2

Jane's assessment tool selection

Assessment Tool	Timetable	Rationale
Reading interview	Independent work time	To become aware of Kamal's perceptions of the reading process and his beliefs about how reading works
Garfield Elementary Attitude Scale	As a part of language arts with a small group	To compare Kamal's attitudes about academic and recreational reading with his peers
IRI	Independent work time	To assess Kamal's print and meaning processing; to determine reading level
Spelling features	As a part of language arts with small group	To assess stage of spelling development

| **ACTIVITY 7.3** | **Analyzing and Interpreting the Reading Behaviors of an Individual** |

(*Note:* You may want to do the case study with a partner.)

What to Do: In this activity you will get into the "thick" of diagnosis. You will need to analyze observations, noting relationships between them and between reading behaviors and the reading process. Next you will interpret your findings, noting patterns of strength and need.

To begin, pretend that a teacher actually administered some of the assessments you suggested for Kamal, and has recorded her observations in the following case study. Carefully examine observations of his oral reading and comprehension as recorded by the teacher.

Next, analyze his reading behaviors by using the accompanying worksheet (Activity 7.2 Worksheet). Record your analyzing or results in the form of summary statements. These are sentences that consolidate what you notice about Kamal's reading and writing. A few examples are provided for you.

Finally, interpret your findings, using your knowledge base (what you know about literacy development and the reading process, and from your own personal experiences). Also record your interpretations in the form of statements; however, recognize that your interpretations synthesize your findings into patterns of reading behavior. Therefore, you are likely to have fewer interpretive statements. Again, some examples are provided to guide your thinking.

Case Study:
Kamal, a Third-Grade Student

Kamal loves video games. He prefers hands-on activities. He likes to be busy doing something. He enjoys ghost stories. He had the book, *Scary Stories 3: More Tales to Chill Your Bones* by Alvin Schwartz (1991), at his desk all year. He often shared stories from this book.

When the teacher gave him an informal reading inventory, his scores showed the following levels:

IRI	Independent	Instructional	Frustration
Word list	grade 1 to 2	2	3
Oral reading	1	2	3
Silent reading	P	1	2 to 3

After reviewing the informal reading inventory and the retellings, Kamal's teacher felt that his retelling was poor—he rarely expressed a main idea and only mentioned a few details. His retellings usually missed the point, shown by the way he reported nonessential, text-based information. He rarely used his own knowledge to interpret the story or associated what he was reading to his own life.

In his oral reading, Kamal's miscues were characterized by being similar at the beginning and ending of the word, but different in the middle. He seldom corrected his miscues, most of which did not make sense in the story.

When surveying his writing, the teacher noticed that Kamal used letters to represent the sounds he heard in words. There were spaces between the words, and Kamal followed a left-to-right sequence in his writing. Sometimes Kamal represented a whole word with a single letter or a group of letters that represented a sound in the word.

In a group situation, the teacher noticed that Kamal was quiet, not offering any response, but rather letting his classmates take the lead.

Analysis and Interpretation Worksheet (Kamal)

Directions: Consider the evidence. Then record statements that convey your analysis and interpretation of Kamal's reading behaviors. Some summary statements have been provided to assist you.

Analysis *(summary statements)*	*Interpretation* *(patterns)*
1. Kamal uses beginning letters to predict unknown words, but does not check for sense.	1. Kamal does not confirm his predictions with the text cues.
2. Kamal relies on others to retell what has been read, although he himself does understand, to some extent, what has been read.	2. He is a dependent reader, relying on others to construct and articulate the meaning for him.
3. He reads orally at the second-grade level, but his silent comprehension is only at the first-grade level.	3.
4. He is in the letter-name stage of spelling development.	
5.	

FOLLOW-UP DISCUSSION

As you probably determined, Kamal is an active learner but doesn't seem to apply many of those active strategies when reading. He does guess at unknown words, probably using much of his background knowledge; however, he doesn't check those guesses. When trying to comprehend a story, he is even less active. It is as if he doesn't understand how to use the process; therefore, his retellings are poor. Writing, too, presents somewhat of a problem.

Although this analysis seems bleak, remember that Kamal is an active learner in other tasks. So, you could start by having Kamal predict story meaning, and then talk about what he knows. This might be the key step he has been missing. However, what you will do with Kamal in the classroom will depend on the other students as well.

So, in the next activity, let's turn our attention to the other students in Kamal's class.

ACTIVITY 7.4   **Analyzing and Interpreting the Reading Behaviors of a Small Group**

(*Note:* Do this activity in four small groups—there should be at least four in each group. Each group will become the expert on one of the students—Diana, Marcus, Joe, or Nicole.)

What to Do First: Because you are going to analyze and interpret the reading behaviors of several children, this activity includes several parts and will take considerable time.

On the next several pages, there are four case studies of Kamal's classmates, Diana (A), Marcus (B), Joe (C), and Nicole (D). First, carefully read each case study, noting interests, attitudes, and reading levels, along with other aspects of the case data. Then analyze and interpret each case, consolidating your thinking into summary statements and patterns of reading behavior. As before, some statements are provided for you. To increase your skill in this area, however, there are fewer completed statements, some statements that need to be completed by you, and still others that need to be generated on your own.

Case Study A: Diana

Diana is extremely quiet and hard to get to know. She is bilingual speaking—Russian in the home and English at school. On the interest inventory, she indicated some interest in Indians. She said that if she could be anything, she would be a bird and would sit in a tree and not come out.

She is quite sophisticated for a third grader, expressing much interest in boys, kissing, makeup, and babies. She does like to read and feels books are great gifts. She enjoys recreational reading, but does not feel positively toward academic reading. She strongly dislikes it when the teacher asks her questions about what she has read.

When her teacher gave Diana an informal reading inventory, her scores showed the following levels:

IRI	Independent	Instructional	Frustration
Word list	P	1	2
Oral reading	P	1	2
Silent reading	P	1	2

After reviewing the informal reading inventory and retellings, Diana's teacher felt that her retelling seemed highly creative, and that Diana was involved with the text; however, her responses did not relate the main idea or important details. She selectively used her own knowledge to elaborate the interesting parts of the story, but not the main points; therefore, her retellings usually missed the mark.

In her oral reading she made only a few miscues, and about half the time these miscues made sense in the context of the selection. Her miscues were usually words that she was unfamiliar with in the English language.

When surveying Diana's writing, the teacher noticed that Diana used many invented spellings, representing every sound heard. Many of the small, high-frequency words such as *we, had,* and *day* were spelled correctly.

Both in the group and alone, Diana does not volunteer answers because she wants to be right. On the informal reading inventory, she would not predict what the story would be about, even though she knew there were no "right" answers.

Analysis and Interpretation Worksheet (Diana)

Directions: Analyze and interpret reading behaviors by completing statements and generating new ones on your own.

Analysis
(summary statements)

Interpretation
(patterns)

1. Diana is bilingual, speaking in Russian only when at home.

1. Diana does not use prediction strategies; she is a low risk-taker.

2. Diana is very concerned about being _____ ; she will not volunteer guesses or answers to questions.

2. Diana's graphophonemic system is well-developed; her _____ system in English needs to be developed further so she can utilize this system as an aid in print and meaning processing.

3. Diana does not contribute her own background knowledge to make _____ .

3.

4. She is at a _____ stage of spelling development.

4.

5. She reads both orally and silently at the _____ level.

6.

Case Study B: Marcus

Marcus is very athletic. He enjoys and participates in hockey, baseball, and karate. He has a positive self-concept. He enjoys writing and willingly shares stories written about himself. He is academically successful in math. However, he has little interest or use for reading. The only reading he does is in school. He doesn't think books are particularly valuable and would never want one as a gift. "It would be embarrassing," he claims.

When the teacher gave him an informal reading inventory, his scores showed the following levels:

IRI	Independent	Instructional	Frustration
Word list	5	6	7–8
Oral reading	2	3	4
Silent reading	1–2	2	3

After reviewing the informal reading inventory and retellings, Marcus's teacher felt that his retelling was somewhat average, but he usually missed the main idea of the selection. He could remember many specific details, but seemed unable to tie them together to form a complete story line. In fact, he seldom used his own knowledge to interpret a story.

In his oral reading, his miscues were few. However, he read slowly, word-by-word, focusing on accurately pronouncing each word. Apparently he viewed reading as an activity in which the goal was to say words correctly.

When looking over his writing, the teacher noticed that Marcus used an occasional invented spelling, but he usually used a visual strategy where every letter in a word was represented. Many of the words were spelled correctly.

In a group situation, Marcus always related information about the story and was eager to discuss what he remembered, particularly specific details.

Analysis and Interpretation Worksheet (Marcus)

Directions: Analyze and interpret reading behaviors by completing statements and generating new ones on your own.

Analysis
(summary statements)

Interpretation
(patterns)

1. Marcus possesses a large sight vocabulary, but does not apply _____ .

1. Marcus may be too word-dependent, which leads to reading as a word-calling activity rather than a meaning-making one.

2. Marcus has well-developed knowledge of the graphophonemic system.

2.

3.

3.

4. He reads well orally, but his retellings _____ .

4. Marcus's grasp of the graphophonemic system is age-appropriate.

5. He is in a _____ stage of spelling development.

5.

6.

Case Study C: Joe

According to a survey of reading attitudes and interests, Joe loves reading in school and out. His attitude toward school in general is quite positive.

He enjoys movies and sees them a lot. His favorites include *Dick Tracy, Batman,* and those starring Arnold Schwarzenegger. He talks and writes about these movies often in his journal.

When the teacher gave him an informal reading inventory, his scores showed the following levels:

IRI	Independent	Instructional	Frustration
Word list	1	2	3
Oral reading	1	2	3
Silent reading	1–2	2	3

After reviewing the informal reading inventory and the retellings, Joe's teacher felt that Joe wanted to make meaning and remember what he read; however, what he got from the text was not what it said because Joe overrelied on using what he knew to interpret a story when he could not figure out the words. He often used nonessential information and what he knew to construct a new story. His retellings, however, showed that he could compose a story, making generalizations that could be applied to the real world, and was highly creative in his interpretations.

In his oral reading, Joe used the beginning letters of words to try to figure out unfamiliar ones. He labored over each word, trying hard to decode the words; however, he had few other strategies for figuring out a word. Sometimes this decoding worked, but other times it did not. When he could not decode a word, Joe would skip it and continue to read, struggling to regain meaning and often creating a new meaning.

After reviewing his writing, Joe's teacher noticed that he knew how to spell familiar sight words; otherwise, he used a letter-naming strategy. Sometimes difficult words would be represented by only one or two letters that represented the sounds in the words.

During discussions, Joe often took the lead, using his knowledge of the world to contribute to the discussion.

Analysis and Interpretation Worksheet (Joe)

Directions: Analyze and interpret reading behaviors by completing statements and generating new ones on your own.

*Analysis
(summary statements)*

1. Joe attempts to sound his way through unknown words; this is the only strategy he uses.

2. He is a letter-name speller, e.g., "hechhicking" for "hitchhiking."

3.

4.

*Interpretation
(patterns)*

1. He overrelies on his graphophonemic system to decipher unknown words.

2.

3.

Case Study D: Nicole

Nicole's strong suit is math, which contributes immensely to her confidence as a learner. She has a good attitude toward reading, too, claiming, "Books are neat." She especially enjoys adventure stories. She enjoys most aspects of recreational and academic reading; however, she expresses a strong dislike for workbooks and tests:

When the teacher gave her an informal reading inventory, her scores showed the following levels:

IRI	Independent	Instructional	Frustration
Word list	1	2–3	4
Oral reading	1	2	3
Silent reading	1	2	3

After reviewing the informal reading inventory and retellings, Nicole's teacher felt that Nicole's retellings were sparse. When she got confused about the story, she simply refused to continue the retelling. Her retellings did not include the main idea of the story, but she did relate the details.

In her oral reading, Nicole's miscues were similar at the beginning and ending of the word. However, she seldom corrected her miscues, most of which did not make sense in the story. She read word-by-word, trying to regain the meaning of the story.

Analysis and Interpretation Worksheet (Nicole)

Directions: Analyze and interpret reading behaviors by completing statements and generating new ones on your own.

Analysis
(summary statements)

1. Nicole continues to read even if it does not make sense.

2. She tends to read word-by-word, often substituting words into the sentence that do not make sense.

3.

4.

Interpretation
(patterns)

1. Nicole does not confirm her predictions by using text or context cues.

2.

3.

(*Note:* To continue this activity, regroup so that at least one expert on each student [Kamal, Diana, Marcus, Joe, and Nicole] is in a group.)

What to Do Next: Having analyzed and interpreted each of the case studies, go back and reexamine your worksheets for Kamal, Diana, Marcus, Joe, and Nicole. If possible, lay all the worksheets out before you, searching for commonalities across all five individuals. For example, it appears that all of these students lack fluency in their reading.

In the following space, jot down what you observe to be common patterns of reading behavior for the group as a whole. As you are noting patterns, you may want to add information to your summary statements and interpretations. For instance, one student's behaviors may cause you to ask, "Are there others in the group who exhibit this same behavior?" In answering this question, you may find that you need to add information to the individual worksheets.

As we searched for patterns, we noted eight of them. You may detect a few more or less. To give you some hints, we have provided two that we observed.

Common Patterns Noted in the Data

1. All of the students lack fluency.
2. Joe and Marcus demonstrate greater control of the reading process, because they read for meaning and attempt to integrate their background knowledge with the text.
3.

4.

5.

6.

7.

8.

What to Do Last: To aid you in seeing the group's strengths and needs at a glance, use the common patterns noted in the data to construct a features grid. This grid will be similar to the features matrix you developed in Chapter Three when you were constructing an Assessment Tool Quick Reference Card.

We have already begun a features grid for you. Based on your analysis and interpretation of the reading behaviors of this group, complete the grid by adding more features. Then decide whether each student demonstrates those features. Your resulting grid becomes a way to organize a lot of information into a form that facilitates the instructional decision making which must necessarily follow.

Features Grid

Name	Good attitude	Lacks fluency	Feature Uses what he/ she knows	Controls process	Word caller
Kamal		X			X
Diana		X			
Marcus		X			X
Joe	X	X			X
Nicole	X	X			X

FOLLOW-UP DISCUSSION

Let's review our analysis and interpretation of the reading behaviors of this group. The thematic patterns that emerge appear to be the following:

1. The group as a whole lacks fluency in their reading.
2. The students appear to process meaning better when they read orally, perhaps using their own voices as supports in the meaning construction process.
3. Their sight-word knowledge and reading vocabulary appear limited.
4. All the students demonstrate short attention spans, which distract them from processing print; this shortcircuits meaning construction and, ultimately, control of the overall reading process. The net result is frustration, not satisfaction, with the reading experience.

Joe and Marcus do appear to have a better grasp of the overall reading process than do the others. Perhaps they could assist the others by expressing what they do as readers and modeling predicting, confirming, and integrating behaviors for their peers. In general, it appears the group needs substantial experiences with the reading process as a whole to grasp that it is a meaning-making process, not a performance. Furthermore, short bits of highly motivating text may be needed to keep the group attending to text and focused on meaning processing.

Having analyzed and interpreted data, we turn next to the matter of choosing appropriate instructional techniques. Once we "see" patterns of reading behavior, we can better judge what to do and how to do it in the instructional context. Consequently, the final two activities of this chapter involve you in choosing instructional techniques that sustain strong reader strategies while bolstering those that are weak. For this, you need to put to immediate use that Handbook of Teaching Techniques you developed in Chapters Four and Five. First, we will return to Kamal and decide what to do instructionally with him, then we will conclude with our third-grade group, determining what we will do to enhance their strengths and meet their needs.

Awareness of reading behavior patterns guides the selection of appropriate instructional techniques.

ACTIVITY 7.5

Translating Findings into Instructional Action: Choosing Instructional Techniques and Reader Strategies

(*Note:* Try this activity on your own or with a partner.)

What to Do: In this activity you will return to our third grader, Kamal. Using as a frame of reference the analysis and interpretation you conducted, you will now choose instructional techniques and reader strategies that enhance his reading strengths and address his needs. In addition, you will provide a rationale for why you decide to do what you will do, since it is professionally responsible behavior to support your decisions.

Use the format provided to make your plans and state your rationales. As we often have done before, we have provided you with examples to assist your thinking. When you are finished, take some time to share your ideas with a colleague.

Worksheet for Instructional Techniques/Reader Strategies

Strengths	Techniques/Strategies	Rationale
1. Reads for meaning	ReQuest	Builds on active self-questions, yet shows a model for various types
2.		
3.		

Needs	Techniques/Strategies	Rationale
1. Oral reading	Retrospective repeated readings	Focus on how to use background knowledge and printed context to self-correct miscues
2.		
3.		
4.		

FOLLOW-UP DISCUSSION

Take a moment to compare your ideas with those of Danielle, a soon-to-be elementary school teacher. Her ideas are presented in Figure 7.3.

Like Danielle, you may have decided to include one or two teaching techniques that develop Kamal's print processing strategies: message writing, perhaps, or word sorts where Kamal is asked to organize words according to specific phonic principles.

You also may recall that Kamal likes ghost stories. Capitalizing on his interest, you may have planned a topic study around ghost stories. Perhaps you suggested that Kamal write his own book of ghost stories to tell in the dark. In the process, you could develop Kamal's writing fluency and his speaking confidence by having him, as an "expert," tell stories to a small group. Overall, your choice of techniques should have supported his emerging meaning processing and bolstered his reading accuracy and writing fluency.

Now to close what has become "another think" of quite some depth and substance, we ask you in the final activity to designate instructional techniques and reader strategies for the small group of third graders you are already familiar with. Take some time with them—it is likely that you will encounter children with similar strengths and needs in your future educational work.

FIGURE 7.3
Danielle's sample

Strengths	Techniques/Strategies	Rationale
1. Enjoys scary stories	Introduce him to more materials that are related, yet varied, e.g., poetry (*Halloween*), fiction, nonfiction (survival type)	Capitalize on his interest and expand his genre awareness
2. Positive attitude toward school; well-liked	Use paired reading experiences	Build on his relationships with his peers; enhance his view of reading as a pleasant social activity

Needs	Techniques/Strategies	Rationale
1. More active involvement with text	DR-TA Cloze techniques	Will have to verbalize and be held accountable for confirming predictions; must use integration skills
2. Self-correction	**Central method of word attack**	Needs strategies to attack unknown words that focus on meaning and print cues
3. Advance spelling stage	Write scary stories in journal	Provide ample opportunity to write and explore spellings
4. Main idea selection	Story frame	Provides a graphic framework to help organize thoughts and detect main point of story

ACTIVITY 7.6   **Translating Findings into Instruction for a Group of Third Graders**
(*Note:* Try this activity on your own or with the group of case experts.)

What to Do: As with the case of Kamal, choose instructional strategies and reader strategies for the third-grade group as a whole. Use your analysis and interpretation of their reading behaviors as the basis for your decisions. You may find your features grid useful in overviewing the similarities and differences among these readers.

Use the following worksheet to record your thinking. Be sure to provide a rationale for your instructional decisions. As before, we have provided an example or two to get you started.

Worksheet for Instructional Techniques/Reader Strategies

Strengths	*Techniques/Strategies*	*Rationale*
1. Construct meaning when reading orally	DR-TA	Foster reading for meaning and making predictions using background knowledge
2.		
3.		
4.		

Needs	*Techniques/Strategies*	*Rationale*
1. Lack fluency	Choral reading	Develop accuracy while preserving meaning
2.		
3.		
4.		

FOLLOW-UP DISCUSSION

There should be a match between the identification of reader problems and the teaching techniques and reader strategies selected for use.

This time compare your ideas with the actual teacher of this group. Following in Figure 7.4 is her listing of the group's problems, and the techniques she would consider implementing in her classroom. See how closely your ideas match.

Summary

In this chapter, we spent some time considering how to put diagnosis to work. After reviewing the kinds of decision making that diagnosis entails, you practiced diagnosing by choosing assessment tools and providing a rationale for your choices.

Following this, you went on to the more intense activities of analysis and interpretation. You had an opportunity to exercise your diagnostic skills with an individ-

FIGURE 7.4
Teacher's interpretation and translation of diagnostic information

Problems (Needs)	Techniques/Strategies
Lack fluency	◆ Echo reading ◆ Simultaneous reading/listening ◆ Repeated readings (Choose strategies that involve students reading in a fluent manner with support.)
Develop overall process	◆ DR-TA ◆ Semantic maps ◆ ReQuest (Select strategies that actively engage the students in the process.)
Word callers	◆ Cloze activities ◆ Three-level guides ◆ Graphic organizers (Choose strategies that call for confirmation and integration behaviors.)
Will not risk	◆ ReQuest ◆ Semantic mapping ◆ Word sorts (Develop a nonthreatening environment by offering control to students and ownership for learning.)
Overrely on graphophonemic system	◆ Modified cloze activities ◆ Repeated readings ◆ Predict and confirm (Select strategies that use context clues to identify unknown words.)

ual and with a small group. Finally, you applied your diagnostic insights to the determination of teaching techniques and reader strategies.

Thus, as you may have noticed and as we have implied before, diagnosis and instruction are interrelated; they inform one another. Diagnosis leads instruction, guiding teachers' thoughtful selection of teaching techniques, which activate appropriate and relevant learning experiences. But instruction also leads diagnosis, pointing out new areas for observation and consideration. Recognition of this interdependence of diagnosis and instruction foreshadows the topic of Chapter Eight: reflective teaching.

Further Reading

Barr, R., Sadow, M., & Blachowicz, C. (1990). *Reading diagnosis for teachers* (2nd ed.). New York: Longman. Provides case studies for further practice in diagnostic teaching.

Holdaway, D. (1980). *Independence in reading*. Portsmouth, NH: Heinemann. Presents an individualized approach to reading instruction. The appendices in particular are useful for guiding diagnosis and planning classroom instruction.

Rhodes, L., & Dudley-Marling, C. (1988). *Readers and writers with a difference* (Chapters 7–10). Portsmouth, NH: Heinemann. Describes diagnostically based practices for before-, during-, and after-reading phases of the reading lesson.

Tierney, R., Readence, J., & Dishner, E. (1990). *Reading strategies and practices* (3rd ed.). Boston: Allyn & Bacon. Presents a collection of strategies and techniques, indicating the purpose, rationale, intended audience, description, cautions, and comments with respect to each.

CHAPTER EIGHT

◆

The Reflective Teacher

◆

The important thing is not to stop questioning. Curiosity has its own reason for existing. One cannot help but be in awe when contemplating the mysteries . . . It is enough if one tries merely to comprehend a little of this mystery everyday. Never lose a holy curiosity.
—Albert Einstein

In this book, we have focused on the problem-solving nature of diagnosis, which involves continually questioning what and how we are making decisions about instruction. In Chapter Two we took you through the model of diagnosis, which involves observation, analysis, interpretation, translation, and finally, reflection (see Figure 2.3 in Chapter Two). In Chapter Seven, you used four of these phases to look at specific cases.

In this chapter we want to focus on the last phase, reflection. For each of the diagnosis phases we introduced questions that would help you focus on the critical aspects of the problem you were solving. You observed (gathered information) by asking, "What did I see that was important to students' learning?" You analyzed this information by asking, "How do the different aspects that I see relate?" You interpreted your analysis by asking, "What do these behaviors mean in relationship to reading development and the reading process?" You constructed instructional plans by asking, "What are the best techniques and materials to use with these students?" Now you are ready to look back on the entire event and ask, "What really happened during the lesson?" This is what you do during the reflection phase of diagnosis. You simply step away from the instructional situation and mull over the lesson, integrating what you did, why you did it, what really happened, and what new puzzlements arose. This critical reflection leads to questioning the way in which you solved instructional problems and the assumptions on which you based your decision making. We agree with Einstein; it is important not to stop questioning.

The diagnostic process emphasizes that teaching is not solely the understanding of aspects of the reading process, reading development, and the context of instruction, but is the teacher's willingness to deal with the complexities of these variables within each instructional event. It is important to continually ask questions about the complexities of teaching and to critically reflect on these questions; this leads to tying together the multiple facets of each instructional interaction. Teaching is much more than designing lessons; it involves the combining and recombining of information in order to solve complex problems in a constantly changing environment. Within this environment, teachers figure out solutions to dilemmas and develop justifications for their decisions after considering the various possibilities. Reflection, then, involves reconsidering your actions in order to clarify and expand your knowledge about teaching and to improve student learning. Teachers who engage in this ongoing internal dialogue about how past instruction affected student learning produce higher student achievements (Brophy, 1984).

It is important to continually ask questions about the complexities of teaching and then to critically reflect on these questions, tying together the multiple facets of each instructional interaction.

At every step, teachers reflect on and adjust their teaching. As they encounter problem situations, they reflect as they teach and decide whether to continue their instructional plan or revise it. After this decision is made, instruction continues. When the lesson is complete, teachers will think about what happened, reframing and rethinking the problem situation. This thinking reconstructs the instructional event in order to scrutinize the situation, the rationales for actions, and the personal assumptions about teaching and learning. This leads to new questions and then the cycle begins anew.

As you cycle through this process, you will find yourself immersed in teaching, then have to distance yourself in order to analyze what happened. This distancing helps you reconsider your reasons for a particular instructional plan. Thus, after teaching, you will evaluate the lesson and the modifications that you made. You will think about what specific parts of the lesson produced the desired reading behavior. Then you will reflect about these adjustments and how they fit into the overall diagnostic plan, that is, how the plans, adjustments, and observations operated in concert. But your reflections will not stop. You will continue to distance yourself, just as other teachers do.

> As you cycle through the process, you will find yourself immersed in teaching, and then have to distance yourself in order to reflect about what happened.

Teachers also think about their interactions with students. They think about the amount of support the students need to understand the lesson. They think about specific prompts, such as, "What do you know about the . . . ?" or perhaps other scaffolds, like "I believe the author wants you to think about the. . . ." that they used to promote active reading. Critical to reflecting is how teachers evaluate their own natural responses that occurred during the lesson.

Teachers that continue to grow in their own knowledge of teaching expand the reflective process even further. After teaching, they not only think about the actual event—including their intuitive adjustments, their observations, and their original plan—but they also think about their rationales for the plans. Thus, reflective teachers cross-check their practice with their theories. They realize that many of their intuitive adjustments come from their complex network of knowledge and beliefs. This network undergirds the rationales for their instructional decision making.

> Reflective teachers realize that many of their intuitive adjustments come from their complex network of knowledge and beliefs.

In this practice vis-à-vis theory thinking, teachers reflect on how an instructional event brought to students a new understanding of the reading process, as well as how the event affected a specific child's reading development. Through the reflective process, teachers are continually elaborating and changing their personal assumptions about the reading process.

Education students have begun reflecting on their own teaching, and these reflections have informed their lesson planning as well as their theory of reading. The following activities include the reflections of novice teachers working with students who have reading problems. You will read through the reflections, and then analyze the statements using the cycle of reflection: (1) confronting a problem situation, (2) reframing and rethinking the problem, (3) resolving the problem, and (4) thinking about how the problem was resolved.

| **ACTIVITY 8.1** | **Looking Inside the Minds of Novice Teachers** |

(*Note:* Do this with a partner.)

What to Do: Read each reflective statement and the background. Think about what might have happened during instruction, and create a mental picture of the instructional situation. Discuss this picture with your partner. Following this, discuss with your partner the questions that follow each reflective statement, then jot down your answers. Read the section, "Expanding the Reflection," then respond to the "On Your Own" section that follows.

Statement 1:
Steve Is Thinking about Adjustments

Background

Steve, Amanda's teacher, is an avid reader and believes that all people are active thinkers who make predictions and guesses about their environment as well as about what they read. Amanda is a challenge to teach. She is a fourth-grade girl who can read words readily and fluently. She likes to read orally because she has wonderful intonation and inflections. However, she has difficulty understanding what she is reading and doesn't know how to construct meaning while she is reading. She is very quiet and extremely passive, preferring not to make guesses or take risks. She seldom uses what she knows, but instead repeats exactly what is in the text. Steve decided to use a story map during the new text portion of instruction to allow Amanda to demonstrate her strengths (repeating what the text says). This is the fourth story map they have worked on together.

Steve's Reflection

During the lesson, I put the story map away and modeled self-questioning (how to use what I know and what the text says to predict and revise), especially prediction. I used the story map as a summary tool after the lesson. I liked the modification. As a result, today Amanda elaborated and answered the comprehension questions by using her background knowledge. I am much happier with her progress.

Questions

1. What problem did Steve confront in his teaching?

2. What indicated that Steve was rethinking his problem?

3. What did Steve do to resolve the problem?

4. How did Steve connect his thinking? (Did he connect his actions with the student's behavior?)

5. What do you think Steve has changed or elaborated in his personal theory about reading comprehension? About prediction?

Expanding This Reflection

Steve reflected on the adjustment he made as he taught. Thus, he consciously made a change during his instruction. In other words, what was happening instructionally was not getting the desired result of helping Amanda elaborate and answer comprehension questions. So, in the throes of teaching, he reflected-in-action and changed his original plan. Afterwards, he wrote down how the adjustment affected Amanda's reading. (As a result, she elaborated and answered the comprehension questions by using her background knowledge.) However, he did not write down why the story map wasn't working. He probably thought about it, but did not write it down. Writing the reflection down provides a diagnostic record of observations and reflections that becomes part of the diagnostic information upon which the teacher can make decisions.

On Your Own

Pretend you are Steve, and when you tried the self-questioning, it didn't work. Amanda just sat and looked at you. You were doing all the work. Write down the adjustments you might have made.

Statement 2:
Betty Is Thinking about Scaffolds

Background

Betty, Carmen's teacher, believes that all children are risk-takers who enjoy a natural curiosity about print and meaning. She believes that all some children need is a simple example along with some encouragement to use this process with print. Carmen is a second-grade girl who sounds out words easily but reads very slowly, almost word-by-word. Betty is puzzled, because Carmen does not understand anything that she reads silently and very little of what she reads orally. It is as if reading aloud is all there is to reading. Betty thought that she needed to help Carmen learn to use her background knowledge to predict. This would help both her comprehension and fluency. During the skill and strategy instruction, Betty focused on self-directed questioning, especially prediction. Betty consciously modeled and supported Carmen's efforts in using this active process.

Betty's Reflection

I could tell Carmen was trying hard to predict. I kept trying to bring different ideas to the surface for her to use. During the next week, I had to model continuously to try to explain the process of betting or predicting. During the third week, I couldn't believe the improvement on prediction. I need to model and model! She has ideas, but seems scared because they may not be correct. I tell her it's just a guess or bet. She then relaxes and takes a risk (Walker, 1992b).

Questions

1. What problem did Betty confront in her teaching?

2. What indicated that Betty was rethinking the problem?

3. What did Betty do to resolve the problem?

4. How did Betty connect her thinking? (Did she connect her actions with the student's behavior?)

5. What do you think Betty has changed or elaborated in her personal theory about reading comprehension? About prediction?

Expanding This Reflection

Betty reflected on the modeling and scaffolds needed to help Carmen take risks as she read. She initially thought that Carmen would readily take risks once shown an example of what a prediction was. However, this was difficult for Carmen, because she wanted to always be right. So Betty modeled frequently, and encouraged Carmen by making suggestions. Betty certainly wrote about the connection between what she did and Carmen's risk-taking behaviors. This writing helped her rethink her ideas about all students being natural risk-takers. She began thinking that maybe the situation and the nature of the task had a lot more to do with taking risks than she first thought.

On Your Own

Pretend you are Betty, and when you tried the self-questioning, Carmen could predict but she seldom revised her prediction, even when it was obvious that her prediction was way off base. Write down what scaffolds you might use.

Statement 3:
Gary Is Thinking about Changing Plans

Background

Gary, Kevin's teacher, is an active reader and writer who likes reading orally. He has presented several Readers Theatre scripts in his college classes. Kevin is a third grader who comprehends stories fairly well. However, learning to correctly identify words has been very difficult for him. His oral reading is marked with long pauses as he figures out words. Sometimes, instead of pausing, he will repeat a word two or three times while he figures out the next word. His difficulty in quickly identifying words is reflected in his spelling development. Although he is reading near the third-grade level, he still uses many invented spellings. Gary has been working on fluency during skill and strategy instruction.

Gary's Reflection

Kevin seems to be grouping words in phrases today. In fact, the procedure where I modeled my phrasing and Kevin followed has helped both his fluency and comprehension. I think it is time to change. Since he likes to make up endings to stories, but he uses a lot of invented spellings for a third grader, I think I will have him do some writing. This will work on both his meaning and print processing.

Next day: I'm sure glad I used the guided imagery with the writing. I had Kevin read his story back to me orally to see if he could read his own writing. He read it fluently. This continued work on fluency and modeling phrases, but in a different manner.

Questions

1. What problem did Gary confront in his teaching?

2. What indicated that Gary was rethinking the problem?

3. What did Gary do to resolve the problem?

4. How did Gary connect his thinking? (Did he connect his actions with the student's behavior?)

5. What do you think Gary has changed or elaborated in his personal theory about reading fluency? About writing?

Expanding This Reflection

Gary believed he needed to change the direction of his lessons. The procedure of modeling a phrase and then having Kevin follow the model had helped Kevin's fluency, so Gary began to work on spelling development, which in turn would help the word identification. Notice how Gary related Kevin's spelling development to his reading performance when deciding to work on this particular skill. Gary also suggested that writing a story ending could work on two goals at once (print and meaning processing). This shows that Gary thought about how activities interrelate and that they can be used to work on several reading concerns at once.

On Your Own

Pretend you are Gary, and when you tried the **guided imagery** and story writing, it didn't work. Kevin said, "I didn't make any pictures in my mind, so I don't have anything to write." Write down what you might say and do.

FOLLOW-UP DISCUSSION

As you read these reflections, you looked inside the minds of beginning teachers, like yourself, who are struggling to develop reading lessons that promote active meaning construction. These practicing teachers observed their students during instructional events, and, from these observations, began to analyze and interpret what they observed. These reflections were written down after each instructional session so they could provide a narrative of problems encountered in their teaching as well as possible solutions.

As these practicing teachers stepped back from the instructional events, they thought about the congruence between their original plans, the adjustments they made, the support they provided, and what they observed. These reflections led them to ask new questions and develop reasons for changing and adjusting their original plan.

As you can see, writing your reflections is an integral part of your growth as a teacher. Each day you need to record your plans and write reflections about your teaching. These thoughts inform your practice as you create lesson plans based on a reflective analysis of the lesson.

As you teach, your observations and reflections will inform your teaching and, although the basic rationale for selecting a particular instructional technique may remain somewhat the same, your rationales for this selection will change as you reflect on your theory of the reading process, reading development, and instructional situation. Therefore, equally important to the process of reflection is the rethinking of your theory or guiding principles.

ACTIVITY 8.2	**Writing a Reflection**

(*Note:* Do this on your own)

What to Do: Think about one of the lessons you have conducted in this class. Bring to class your plans and any of your reactions after instruction. Focus on one aspect of the lesson that presented a challenge to you. Then, think about what the problem was, and rethink the situation. As you begin rethinking the problem, write down your thinking. This is *reflection-on-action*. Answer the following questions about your thinking.

1. What problem did you confront in your teaching?

2. What triggered your rethinking of the problem?

3. What did you do to resolve the problem?

4. Did you connect any aspects of your thinking? (Did you connect your actions with changes in the student's behavior, student's literacy development, text characteristics, situation, the task?)

5. Did you change or elaborate your personal theory about reading or writing?

FOLLOW-UP DISCUSSION

What did you find out about your teaching? As you rethought aspects of the lesson and your interactions with the students, you engaged in *reflection-on-action*. Your thoughts might have centered on changes in your plans or on elaborating your own theory of reading. We have found that some of the teachers in our classes have created their theories as they reflected on the lesson after it was completed. Whatever your thoughts after instruction, the more you engage in reflection-on-action—which occurs after you teach—the more likely it is that you will reflect *in* action and change your course of action to meet student needs while you are teaching. Remember, research shows that teachers who reflect during and after instruction produce higher achievement in their students (Brophy, 1984).

Summary

In this chapter we have focused on using the reflective process to inform your instruction and your theories about reading. After teaching, you are encouraged to mentally reconstruct what happened and reflect on the instructional event. As you reframe the problem situation, you need to consider a variety of alternatives and anticipate the consequences of each scenario. Reflecting involves confronting a complex and dynamic situation, thinking and rethinking the various complexities of the situation, and then basing decisions on your assumptions about teaching and learning. Reflection will lead you to propose a tentative solution or plan, while at the same time constructing a modified rationale based on the instructional event and your assumptions. This rethinking often results in changing and refining your understanding of the reading process. As you use the analytic process to develop and change your instruction, you will find that this reflective process is critical to your own personal development as a teacher.

Further Reading

Clift, R. T., Houston, W. R., & Pugach, M. C. (Eds.). (1990). *Encouraging reflective practice in education: An analysis of issues and programs* (pp. 20–38). New York: Teachers College Press. Includes chapters of various authors explaining frameworks for developing reflective practice in preservice teacher education.

Grimmett, P. P., & Erickson, G. L. (Eds.). (1988). *Reflection in teacher education.* New York: Teachers College Press. Includes chapters that explain different points of view about what reflection is and how it influences teaching.

Schon, D. (1987). *Educating the reflective practitioner.* San Francisco: Jossey-Bass. Discusses reflection-in-action that frames many of the decisions teachers make.

Walker, B. J. (1990). A model for diagnostic narrative in teacher education. In N. Padak, T. Rasinski, U. J. Logan (Eds.), *Challenges in reading* (pp. 1–10). Provo, UT: College Reading Association. Presents a model for developing reflective thinking in preservice teachers.

PART FOUR

Managing Diagnostic Information

In Part Four, we examine two areas that powerfully influence the application of the diagnostic process and of diagnostic procedures in classrooms. One of these areas is formal assessment or standardized testing. Testing is a reality of school life; when properly understood and appropriately used, it can enlarge our understanding of the reader's achievements. The other area is the important skill of information management. Without it, both the formal and informal data we gather and interpret may not be successfully translated into day-to-day instructional practices.

We begin in Chapter Nine with a brief discussion of standardized assessment, comparing it to a camera "snapshot." We then involve you in a number of activities that allow you to explore the use of standardized testing in understanding reading behaviors. And finally, we engage you in some decision making that concretely makes our point: Standardized assessment is most useful when used in combination with informal assessment. Together these create a powerful lens for observing what readers can do, enlightening our understanding of how to further their growth.

In Chapter Ten we address the very practical issue of organizing and managing diagnostic information from multiple sources. What reading information to collect and when and where to store it are also realities of school life. Following a short discussion of fundamentals associated with data collection and organization, we present three information management systems for your consideration. At particular points in the school year, any one of these may serve as a mechanism for decision making with respect to an individual child's achievement in reading. For the moment, we invite you to select one system and then provide reasons for your choice.

As in previous chapters, we close with a few suggested readings. We have included them to encourage you to continue your exploration and study of these two important topics. As realities of schooling, they continuously demand our thoughtful attention and well-informed consideration.

CHAPTER NINE

◆

Using Standardized Assessments

◆

Standardized assessment is the science of strange behaviors of children in strange situations with strange adults for the briefest possible periods of time.
—Peter Johnston

In the preceding chapters we focused on informal assessments that used natural situations, rather than "strange" ones, to help children actively construct meaning. For example, we suggested using retellings as an assessment tool. Retelling is a natural activity; much of life involves relating what we have read and what our experiences are. In social situations, people often retell newspaper articles or magazine articles as a way of communicating information and clarifying their ideas. When we assess retelling, we are watching the process of constructing meaning. It is like videotaping the constructive process. In fact, many informal assessments are much like videotapes in that they allow us to watch readers construct responses.

Standardized or formal assessments, on the other hand, are more like camera "snapshots," freezing a specific action at one moment in time. As testing tools, they are used to describe specific reading behaviors connected with a prescribed task at one point in time. These behavioral responses are then examined in relation to a normative or representative group of readers.

In this book, you have begun to look closely at children's literate behaviors. In your looking, you have learned to analyze and interpret these behaviors, translating your interpretations into plans to teach children to be active learners in their classrooms. These assessment notions are based on Vygotsky's concept of the "zone of proximal development," or that range in which the teacher, using scaffolds such as leading questions, cooperative tasks, prompts, or modeling, moves the learner to a more challenging task (Vygotsky, 1978). We have also stressed evaluating what learners can do rather than what they can't do. The assessments used in such evaluations result in descriptions of the ways individual students learn as they are assisted in completing challenging tasks. Consequently, this "natural" approach to assessment reveals a richer profile of individual readers than does a "snapshot" approach to assessment.

However, as a teacher, you will also collect data from large-scale achievement tests and psychoeducational batteries, so it is important to understand standardized assessment along with informal assessment. Large-scale achievement tests, such as the *Gates-MacGinitie Reading Test* (1989), or a standardized assessment used by psychologists, such as the *Woodcock-Johnson Psychoeducational Battery* (1977), are "snapshots" of performance, reflecting an episodic rather than a continuous approach to assessment. Characteristically, they sample behavior on a specific task for a short period of time.

Informal assessments are much like videotapes. They allow us to watch how readers construct a response.

Standardized or formal assessments are like camera "snapshots," freezing specific actions at one moment in time.

The zone of proximal development is the range in which the teacher uses scaffolds to help the learner negotiate more challenging tasks.

173

Standardized assessments are developed on different principles than are informal assessments. In informal assessments, we choose activities where we can observe a student's literate behaviors. Because standardized assessment is based on a representative group of learners that have all participated in the same task, these assessments use items in which reading performance can be predicted in a prescribed way. Standardized assessments rely on tasks that can be scored objectively, that are valid (the test measures what it says it measures), and that are reliable (the test result can be duplicated). With these conditions in mind, standardized assessments focus on a product of reading, such as scores on multiple-choice tests after reading a paragraph, or the number of words recognized on sight. In many standardized assessments, children read short, densely written paragraphs. They may understand only about half of each paragraph, but these scores are averaged together to create a score that is then evaluated in relation to the representative sample (normal curve). This normal curve means that 68% of students in a certain age group or grade level will fall within the average range. This type of assessment is more appropriate for measuring groups of children to help teachers and administrators make judgments about local and state curricula rather than to help them make judgments about individual children.

Psychoeducational assessments, on the other hand, are standardized but individually administered. This type of standardization usually features contrived reading tasks that easily can be measured with a score. These scores then are compared to those of other children in the representative sample; therefore, these assessments also tend to focus on the product of reading rather than on the process. They result in a "snapshot" of a learner's reading performance on a contrived task.

Looking at the purposes and uses of formal assessments is critical, since these tools also inform our work. In the following activities, you are given ample opportunity to explore a number of aspects of formal assessments. More particularly, you will

1. generate a few characteristics of standardized assessments;
2. practice interpreting the results of standardized tests;
3. examine how to use formal assessment tools along with the more informal ones you know; and
4. learn how to make sense of individual psychoeducational assessment data.

As you work through these activities, you will become aware of the many positive features of standardized assessment tools and how they, too, yield information about readers' capabilities and achievements. Moreover, you will also observe that when used jointly, formal and informal assessments provide a powerful lens for looking at what readers can already do, while pointing out where they yet may go.

ACTIVITY 9.1	**Comparing and Contrasting Active Readers and Standardized Test Information**

(*Note:* Do this in a small group.)

What to Do First: For a moment, think back to Chapter One where we examined the reading process. Remember, for example, how we observed that readers bring something to the printed page, using their own background knowledge to make "guesses" about the print. Recalling what readers tend to do, in the provided space jot down a few characteristics of active reading. Of course, feel free to refer back to Chapter One as needed.

Characteristics of Active Reading

What to Do Next: Now, think about all the standardized achievement tests you have taken throughout your academic career. Recall, for instance, having to select main ideas from what seemed an endless number of disconnected paragraphs in what seemed a very limited amount of time. Thinking back to some of these experiences, augment your listing of active reading characteristics by adding information that you might obtain from standardized tests performances.

Information from Standardized Achievement Tests

FIGURE 9.1
Venn diagram

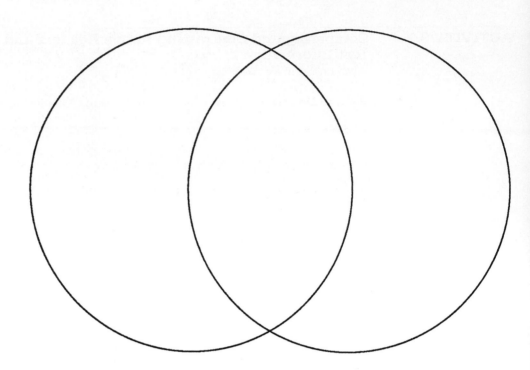

What to Do Last: Using the Venn Diagram in Figure 9.1, indicate the similarities and differences between your two lists: characteristics of active readers and information from standardized tests. Write the similarities in the area where the two circles overlap, and the differences in the arcs where they do not overlap. Think for a moment about the implications of your observations.

FOLLOW-UP DISCUSSION

Before we go on, let's check to see how we compare. How closely does your Venn Diagram resemble ours, shown in Figure 9.2?

FIGURE 9.2
Completed Venn diagram

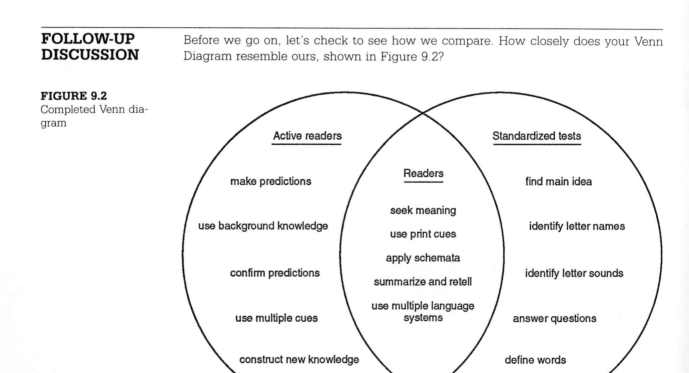

From this first activity, you probably can begin to see why people tend to be dissatisfied with the results of standardized tests. While useful in a rather general way, this form of assessment provides only a snapshot of the reader at a particular time, under specific conditions. It reveals little about the reader and how she is reading, that is, how she processes print and meaning.

This is not to say that standardized assessments have no value. Indeed, they do. When we are interested in large-scale trends, general patterns of achievement, and broad-based literacy status, formal measures are useful and appropriate. As snapshots, they acquaint us with the most general of reader characteristics, for example, decoding skills. Moreover, standardized measures are a reality in most regular classrooms, compensatory reading programs, and special education programs. In fact, they have become a mainstay, and teachers are asked to use them as one means of reporting students' progress.

Since you will soon assume a teaching role, you need a basic understanding of standardized tests and how to inform others about their results. To assist you in this important matter, we invite you to participate in the next activity, where you will be asked to analyze standardized test results. While perhaps a bit intimidating at first, you may find interpreting standardized test data less complicated than your earlier experiences with informal assessment findings.

ACTIVITY 9.2   ## Making Sense of Standardized Test Data

(*Note:* Do this activity in five groups. Each group will look at a different student's progress, then join the other groups to discuss these cases.)

What to Do First: Read the following case study. Examine the data carefully. Think about what the students' scores might mean about their reading performance.

Case Study:
Barbara Uses the *Gates-MacGinitie Reading Test* (1989)

Barbara just completed scoring the *Gates-MacGinitie Reading Test* taken by a small group of her third-grade students. She compiled the scores of the vocabulary test, in which the students read a short word stem and were asked to guess at the word meaning. Next, she compiled the scores for reading comprehension, in which her students read short, unrelated paragraphs silently and then answered literal and inferential questions found in the text. Barbara then transposed these raw scores to standardized scores by using the normative tables found in the manual. The students' standardized scores reflected how they performed in relation to a representative sample of other third graders. Barbara decided to organize these data according to the percentile and grade equivalent table in the manual. In Figure 9.3, the data are reported in percentiles and grade equivalents.

What to Do Next: Flip back to the lists you made in Activity 9.1 about the characteristics of active readers and about information gained from standardized tests. Scan them quickly.

Using this information as a frame of reference, complete the following chart. List one fact about each student's reading. Then generate a hypothesis (an informed guess) about that reader based on the standardized information provided. Again, think about your listing of the characteristics of active readers and of standardized tests; then, from this assessment, list one fact and a hypothesis about each student.

Name	Fact	Hypothesis
Kamal		
Diana		
Marcus		
Joe		
Nicole		

FIGURE 9.3
Gates-MacGinitie (Stan-
dardized) test data

	Vocabulary		Comprehension	
	Percentile	Grade Equivalent	Percentile	Grade Equivalent
Kamal	31	2.5	10	1.7
Diana	4	1.5	5	1.5
Marcus	76	4.1	54	3.2
Joe	16	2.0	31	2.5
Nicole	31	2.5	16	2.0

What to Do Next: Select a student for your work group from those listed. Review the standardized tests data, as well as the fact and hypothesis you generated about your student. Based on this information and your own experiences, jot down your ideas about what instructional techniques you might use with the student. Record your information in the following chart.

Student:

Standardized test results:

Fact(s):

Hypothesis:

Suggested instructional techniques/approaches:

What to Do Last: Join with the other groups in your class. Allow each group to share both its charts—the one that indicates facts and hypotheses about all the students, and the one that lists potential instructional techniques/approaches.

Using the following chart, list the commonalities in each area noted by all the groups. Then share and record problems you encountered in interpreting and translating the standardized test data.

<h3 style="text-align:center">Commonalities</h3>

Hypothesis

Instructional techniques

Problems

FOLLOW-UP DISCUSSION

Your experiences in this activity reacquainted you with some of the characteristics of standardized tests and the data they provide. While you may have recognized much about standardized tests with which you are familiar, you may have encountered difficulty in planning an instructional program around their results. In fact, you may have been a bit uncomfortable making instructional decisions based on seemingly "slim" evidence of reading behavior. You had some information (a score), but you were perhaps unsure of its validity. You may have even asked yourself, "If circumstances were different, would these children have done otherwise?"

As we discussed in the introduction to this chapter, formal or standardized test data are useful in some ways and lacking in others. The data they provide get us in the ballpark, so to speak, but they do not tell us much about how to play. They indicate, in general, the level at which a reader is performing, but they provide few clues as to how. If we are to assist readers so that they can grow in their reading skills, we simply need more information than standardized tests alone can provide. In short, we need multiple indicators of performance—a point we made in Chapter Two when you began your study of reading diagnosis.

Putting this idea of "multiple indicators of performance" to work, in the next set of activities we involve you in using standardized assessment data in conjunction with observations from informal assessments. You will have an opportunity to examine readers' behaviors from more than one source, coordinating them to create a richer description of how and at what level they read. As a result, you may recognize the importance of multiple views of readers' performance; in tandem, these views provide a more powerful lens for observing and understanding readers' behavior.

Standardized assessments indicate, in general, at what level a reader is performing, but they provide few clues as to *how* the reader is performing.

ACTIVITY 9.3 Using Formal and Informal Assessments

(*Note:* Do this activity in five groups, with each group continuing to analyze the same student from the previous activity.)

What to Do First: To begin this activity, locate the summary statements derived from the informal assessments that you made about Kamal, Diana, Marcus, Joe, and Nicole in Chapter Seven. Then locate the hypotheses you generated about these students based on formal assessments in the previous activity. Lay out the information from these two sources side-by-side and study it a bit. In the following chart, jot down what you notice as similarities and discrepancies between the two sources.

Comparing Summary Statements and Hypotheses

Similarities   *Discrepancies*

What to Do Next: Recall Barbara, the third-grade teacher you met earlier. For a moment, pretend you are Barbara and that the different parents of our five children have just received standardized assessment reports in the mail. Each wants you to interpret the report with respect to their children.

In your group, discuss what you might say to the parents. Following your discussion, record two key points you would make about each student. Then JIGSAW with the other groups, in which you create new groups so that each group includes at least one expert on each case study. Share your comments about each of the students.

What would you say to Kamal's parents?

What would you say to Diana's parents?

What would you say to Marcus's parents?

What would you say to Joe's parents?

What would you say to Nicole's parents?

FOLLOW-UP DISCUSSION

Reflect for a moment about how you arrived at what you would say to the parents of these children. Like many teachers, you may have found it necessary to augment the standardized assessment results with the more descriptive informal assessment data to be able to communicate effectively and meaningfully.

Once again we find that standardized assessment results provide only snapshots of reading behavior—frozen still lifes of a sort. While they may validate to some extent what readers can do, they are simply inadequate for describing how readers are doing what they are doing in the course of reading on their own. Informal assessments applied to naturally occurring reading situations are more suited to this purpose. However, by merging information from both of these data sources, we can bring greater clarity to our observations while enlarging the scope of our response to readers' behaviors and performances. In short, our use of multiple sources improves our communication, facilitating our efforts to translate our diagnoses to others.

Let's return at this point to Barbara. Following her discussion with Kamal's parents, she decided that her understanding of Kamal's reading would benefit from further evaluation activities. She was still puzzled about how he processed print and meaning, and what implications his reading difficulties might have on his more general classroom behaviors. As a result of the parent conference, Barbara referred Kamal for further assessment by the school psychologist.

In the next activity you will join Barbara, sharing in her decision-making processes with respect to Kamal. From this experience you will become acquainted with psychoeducational assessment data and how it provides another point of reference about a reader's behaviors.

ACTIVITY 9.4   **Making Sense of Psychoeducational Data**

(*Note:* Do this in your groups.)

What to Do First: Continue reading the case study of Barbara. Why do you think she was puzzled about Kamal? When you finish reading and considering this case, discuss it with your group.

Case Study

Barbara, Kamal's teacher, was puzzled by Kamal's reading performance. He had plenty of background knowledge and he could decode words well. She knew he was fairly nonfluent, but all third-grade students need work on fluency. Kamal, however, was also having difficulty completing classroom assignments. He often would forget to hand in assignments unless she reminded him many times. Sometimes she even called his parents so they could work with him at home. However, all this hand holding hadn't seemed to help. During the parent conference, Kamal's parents expressed concern over his lack of attention and follow through on difficult tasks. Barbara and his parents decided to have Kamal evaluated by the school psychologist, who then administered the *Weschler Intelligence Scale for Children - Revised* (WISC-R) (1974); the *Woodcock-Johnson Psycho-Educational Battery - Part 2* (1977); the *Wide Range Achievement Test - Revised* (Jastak & Jastak, 1984); the *Peabody Picture Vocabulary Test - Revised* (Dunn & Dunn, 1981); and the *Bender Visual-Motor Gestalt Test for Children* (1962). All these assessments, except the Bender Visual-Motor Gestalt Test, are based on normative samples and follow standard procedures.

All of these assessments were administered in a one-to-one setting and the school psychologist followed the prescribed format for administering each task. Kamal's scores are displayed in Figure 9.4. (In the parentheses are specific explanations to help your interpretations.)

From these results, the school psychologist maintained that Kamal has average intelligence and is only slightly behind his peers in reading performance. However, the school psychologist pointed out that Kamal's visual motor ability is greatly impaired and is interfering with both his writing and spelling. The tests show that so far this weakness has not interfered with his reading performance, but it might account for the slow reading rate that Barbara reported. The school psychologist also pointed out that his inattention seems to be a concern from the classroom observations, the parents' report, and from a few indicators on the WISC-R.

Although Barbara knows that Kamal is performing only slightly below grade level, she wonders how he will survive in the fourth grade where he has to read in the content-area textbooks and complete lengthy written assignments on his own.

As a classroom teacher, she has different information about Kamal. In the classroom, he is very social; however, when he reads orally, he does so very slowly, reading word-by-word. Content-area textbooks will certainly be a problem because of his slow reading and poor attention (skimming demands a lot of attention). Additionally, his writing is very slow and he avoids writing whenever possible.

What to Do: Barbara needs your help. With your group, brainstorm possible plans of action. For example, is Kamal a candidate for a special education program? Should a Child Study Team be convened to examine his case? Or would an adjustment in the reading curriculum more adequately address Kamal's needs? What do you think? On a separate piece of paper, describe your position. Be sure to consider multiple sources of information to formulate your position.

FIGURE 9.4
Kamal's psychoeduca-
tional assessment data

Kamal—age 9

WISC-R (Wechsler Intelligence Scale for Children-Revised)

This is a norm-referenced test of general intellectual functioning. It samples performance on verbal tasks (tapping language use) and performance tasks (tapping visual understanding) that yield a full scale score for intellectual functioning. The test has a mean of 100, with average scores spanning from 85 to 115.

Standard Scores
Full Scale Score—98
Verbal Score—112
Performance Score—87

Woodcock-Johnson Psycho-Educational Battery (Part 2—Achievement)

This is an individually administered, norm-referenced test designed to diagnose a student's mastery of various academic subjects. The reading cluster consists of three subtests—letter-word identification, word attack, and passage comprehension.

Grade Level Equivalents
Reading   2.3 (strong word identification)
Math   3.5
Written Language   1.9
Knowledge   5.2

Wide Range Achievement Test-Revised

The reading subtest consists of letter recognition, letter naming, and isolated reading of words on a page. No information is gathered regarding students' oral reading accuracy or comprehension.

Grade Equivalents
Reading   2.7
Math   2.8
Spelling   2.1

Peabody Picture Vocabulary Test-Revised

In this individually administered test, students are asked to select one picture from four to represent the target word. This measures a student's receptive vocabulary, or those words she can recognize in a pictorial rendition. Raw scores are converted to normative data by using standard scores with a mean of 100 and scores in the average range span from 85 to 115.

Standard Score—103

Bender Visual-Motor Gestalt Test

In this individually administered test, students copy nine geometric designs that are then scored to give an age equivalent score for visual-motor integration.

Age Equivalent—6 years

FOLLOW-UP DISCUSSION   Although we now have multiple data sources about Kamal, many of you have very different questions and solutions about what to do. This is not unlike all teaching situations. It is only as we work together and analyze all the possible contingencies that the appropriate placements can be made. Many of the very different solutions may work, but what is interesting is that the test data become only a minor part of the decision making. It is vital to have accurate assessments, but it is not the assessments that make teaching work. It is teachers, parents, specialists, and administrators working together who make the data meaningful. As the placement decision is made, teachers and specialists who are constantly assessing Kamal's progress and making adjustments in the instructional plan are those that help make Kamal's educational experience successful. They create a coherent plan and make it work.

Summary

Peter Johnston characterized standardized assessment as "strange." Through the activities in this chapter, we attempted to make this reality of schooling more friendly and less "strange."

You began by sharing what you already know about standardized assessments from your professional and personal experiences. When comparing this information with the characteristics of informal assessment, you began to see the advantages of both. Standardized tools provide "snapshots" of performance and tend to be product-oriented, while informal tools provide "videos" of readers' behavior and are more process-oriented. In combination, these sources of information create a powerful lens for examining what readers can do.

Following this introduction, you were presented with case studies that asked you to use your understanding of the reading process and of assessments to (1) interpret standardized tests to parents, and (2) to make a decision about special education placement. In these dilemmas you examined not only data, but also your beliefs about assessment, pull-out programs for special services, and reading problems. Realizing the complex decision making you will experience as you teach will make you more receptive to collaborating with other professionals, so that the most appropriate instructional programs can be developed for all children.

Further Reading

Farr, R., & Carey, R. (1986). *Reading: What can be measured?* (2nd ed.). Newark, DE: International Reading Association. Discusses how reading is measured and how these assessments are used by teachers.

Johnston, P. H. (1983). *Reading comprehension assessment: A cognitive basis.* Newark, DE: International Reading Association. Presents a thorough review of standardized and informal assessment, including the underlying factors in assessment.

Lipson, M. Y., & Wixson, K. K. (1991). *Assessment and instruction of reading disability: An interactive approach.* New York: HarperCollins. The chapter on formal assessment thoroughly reviews many of the diagnostic reading tests, achievement tests, and related areas.

CHAPTER TEN

◆

Organizing and Managing
Diagnostic Information

◆

The truest order is what you already find there
—Fairfield Porter

The organization and management of diagnostic information is essential for successful instruction and learning.

We both enjoy a children's story by Leslie McGuire entitled *This Farm's a Mess* (1981). The gist of the story is that although the farmer has all the right equipment and all the time he needs, very little is accomplished because the place is disorganized. For some of us, this may sound all too familiar!

Likewise, diagnostic teaching easily can slip into disorganization if a system is not set up for organizing and managing diagnostic information. At first, setting up such a system may seem like the easiest task yet, but don't be fooled. Getting, keeping, and using diagnostic data on 25 or so children requires considerable organizational skill.

In this chapter we seek to assist you in developing the skills you will need to organize and manage diagnostic information. We begin with a discussion of some essentials—what to collect, for example, and when. We continue by describing three types of management systems: work folders with checklists, literacy folders, and literacy portfolios. In addition, we discuss how these systems are used for various purposes. Finally, we close by providing you an opportunity to use a literacy folder for different purposes. Throughout, we strive to emphasize that if diagnostic activity is to inform our teaching and benefit students' learning, then both its processes and its products must be organized and managed in meaningful ways.

Before we begin your "information management training," there are a few rules that generally apply when organizing and managing diagnostic information.

Rule 1: Students should assist in organizing and managing diagnostic data.

Students should participate in some way in the organization and management of diagnostic information, contributing to it and becoming informed by it. After all, the information is about them, and they have a right to be aware of its contents, to comment on it, and to understand it.

Rule 2: Be selective. Don't keep everything.

Like most collecting activities, it is easy for diagnostic data collection to get out of control. Once we get started (along with our students), there is a propensity to save everything. Checklists, workbook papers, writing samples, and self-evaluations can mount up, overwhelming even the most organized among us. Be efficient and judicious. A few suggestions for collecting efficiently include:

- ◆ Set specific collection times, for example, October, February, and April.
- ◆ Collect "representative" samples of performance only.

187

Rule 3:   Date all samples. Color code them if possible.

An important reason for collecting and maintaining diagnostic information is to note growth in what learners can do. This is thwarted, of course, if the collected samples are not dated. Date everything that you retain. Moreover, consider color coding them for quick reference. For example, you may choose to use color dots on diagnostic samples—orange for October samples, red for February, and blue for April. Or, you may want to use colored sheets of paper for all work samples—blue in fall, red in winter, and green in spring. Whatever system you devise, it serves as a kind of fail-safe procedure, just in case you inadvertently forget to date a sample.

Rule 4:   Keep diagnostic information in one place.

Most of us have experienced saving something and then not being able to find it when we need it. You do not want this to happen with the diagnostic data you manage. Find a place to keep it all together, preferably not in the students' desks. Consider crates with hanging files, file boxes, a file drawer, a library cart, or something similar, but it should be a place where the information is easily accessible (for you and your students), and all together.

Rule 5:   Treat the information with respect.

Like standardized test scores, which we tend to prize highly, the informal diagnostic information we collect and manage should also be held in high regard as a valuable indicator of performance and achievement. If we do so as teachers, students and their parents will do so as well. By handling the data collection process with thoughtfulness, sensitivity, and respect for its owner, teachers convey the attitude that a learner's performance should be evaluated from multiple sources, not just one.

Having introduced you to the ground rules, so to speak, we are ready to examine the how-to of organizing and managing diagnostic information. We will start with what to collect and end with how to use it for different purposes. As we have done in previous chapters, we will engage you in a series of hands-on activities that involve you in discovering the main points of this important topic. More particularly, through these activities we seek to address the following objectives:

1. to introduce procedures for the ongoing collection of diagnostic information, that is, what to collect and when to collect it.
2. to present three systems for managing diagnostic information in classrooms: the work folder and checklist system, the literacy folder system, and the literacy portfolio system.
3. to invite you to choose one of these systems and to explain your reasons for doing so.

ACTIVITY 10.1 Gathering Diagnostic Information: What and When

(*Note:* Do this activity with a partner.)

What to Do First: In classrooms, diagnostic information is everywhere! Students' journals, reports, compositions, and story maps are all examples of diagnostic information.

Some pieces of diagnostic information may be **process-oriented**; that is, they illustrate how children go about reading—how they predict, confirm, and integrate when they are processing print and meaning. A number of the procedures and techniques you learned in this book can be used to provide information about *how* children read. The predict and confirm technique from Chapter Four is one example. Recording a child's "guesses" while he is engaged in this activity may serve as a sample of how he processes print. The directed reading-thinking activity (DR-TA) is another example. Recording a student's responses from a key selection provides a valuable piece of information that can be used for diagnostic and evaluation purposes. Think-aloud comments and miscue analyses are also examples of diagnostic information that can be used to indicate how children are processing print and meaning.

Process-oriented diagnostic information: Illustrations of how readers read, for example, comments gathered during think-alouds.

Product-oriented diagnostic information: Demonstrations of reader knowledge, processes, skills, and attitudes, for example, a completed story map.

Still other pieces of diagnostic information may be **product-oriented,** meaning they reveal what children can do as readers, that is, the strategies they know and the skills they possess. Observing how a child completes a word sort, for example, might reveal decoding skills, while her performance on a three-level guide might be used to indicate inferencing abilities. Samples of children's work, their story maps, and the questions they ask are all demonstrations of what children can do and can be used to document their developing skills and abilities.

In the following space, use what you have learned about diagnostic assessments, procedures, and techniques—as well as your imagination—to brainstorm specific items you think would be useful as meaningful bits of diagnostic information. Be sure to include both process- and product-oriented pieces. Indicate what you think each piece emphasizes, realizing that some items will apply to both types of information. To stimulate your thinking, a few examples have been provided.

Items to Collect as Diagnostic Information

Item	Process	Product
Audiotape of oral reading	X	
A written retelling of a selection	X	X
Read silently		

What to Do Next: For the moment, select three to five items from your list that you would definitely collect. For example, perhaps you would choose to collect an audiotape of each student's reading, a cloze activity, and a writing sample.

Next, decide when you will collect these items from the students—weekly? Monthly? Every nine weeks? Three times a year?

Then tell why you would collect each item. What is your intent? Why is the item important? What might it reveal about children's reading development?

Using the format in the following space, indicate your plan.

What I Will Collect   *When I Will Collect It*   *Why I Will Collect It*

FOLLOW-UP DISCUSSION

In Chapter Two we made the point that reading behaviors should be observed from more than one data source; multiple indicators of performance are needed to appropriately assess an individual's reading. By making a list of a variety of diagnostic information sources, you are approaching this important goal in teaching. Moreover, by planning *when* you will collect such information, you are moving even closer to making this goal a classroom reality.

Let's take a moment to examine the thinking and planning of another student of reading diagnosis. First, read through Carol R.'s list of the potential sources of diagnostic information she would collect in a third-grade classroom.

Sources of Diagnostic Information

What I Will Collect	When I Will Collect It	Why I Will Collect It
1. Oral reading samples	1 time every nine weeks plus each day informally during reading time	Check print processing
2. Journal entries	2 times every nine weeks	Check fluency and spelling
3. Cloze passages	Every week	Check overall process
4. Story maps	2 times every nine weeks	Check story sense and sequencing
5. Selected workbook pages	Every 2 weeks	Assess skill development
6. Interest inventories	1 time each semester	Check range and frequency
7. Attitude surveys	1 time each semester	Monitor feelings and perceptions
8. Student's choice	1 time every nine weeks	Observe choices

Note: Color code fall samples orange, winter samples red, and spring samples blue.

There are several items in Carol's list that are worth special mention. Note, first, that she has chosen to include writing samples and even story maps. She also included an item she referred to as "Student's choice." This was Carol's way of bringing self-assessment into the collection of diagnostic information. It is an item you may want to include in your list if it is not already there.

Next, examine the timetable Carol has devised for collecting these items. Did you notice that Carol has preselected a few specific times for data collection? In addition, she has established predictable times each week for focused observations of students' reading behaviors during reading time. This allows her, on a fairly regular basis, to collect samples of reading behaviors in the context of classroom reading. As she indicates in her plan, she will color-code the data she collects, using orange for fall samples, red for winter samples, and blue for spring samples. In these ways, she is beginning to organize her data collection for the assessment and evaluation functions it must eventually serve.

As you begin your teaching career, we urge you to collect diverse pieces of diagnostic information on each of your students and to devise a way of managing this collection process. In addition, we encourage you periodically to vary what you collect, experimenting with different items that reflect what children think and do. Repeated readings, illustrations of text, features matrices, and graphic organizers can also be used as sources of diagnostic information and evidence of reading performance.

Develop a system for collecting and maintaining diverse items of diagnostic information.

Deciding what to collect and when are the first steps in organizing and managing diagnostic information. Deciding how to store the collection and how to use it for evaluation purposes are the next steps.

ACTIVITY 10.2	**Selecting a Management System**

(*Note:* Do this activity on your own.)

What to Do: Managing reading information about 25 or so learners can be a daunting task. But two rather simple moves on the teacher's part can make this process less intimidating. One is to select a system and to stick with it long enough to determine its value. The other is to include your students in carrying out the procedures and processes of the system. As the old saying goes, "Many hands make light work," and in this instance we would do well to heed this bit of folk wisdom.

To assist you in choosing a system to use in your classroom, in the following charts we provide brief descriptions of three basic ways to organize and manage diagnostic information. Each description profiles the purposes, materials, general procedures, student involvement, and reporting techniques of a specific system. Study the characteristics of each system. Then compare and contrast the systems using the graphic organizer on page 198. Finally, choose one system that you would use in your classroom and give three reasons why you chose that particular one.

The Work Folder and Checklist System

Purpose

1. To collect samples of students' daily work in reading and writing.
2. To monitor students' performance by using a checklist as a guide for evaluating reading and writing samples.

Materials

Individual student folders (files or two-pocket folders)

A prepared checklist, as illustrated in Figure 10.1

General Procedures

1. Provide each student with a work folder or have students make their own.
2. Have students put selected reading and writing items into the folder on a regular basis. For example, students may put certain reading worksheets in their folders each week.
3. Collect the folders on a regular basis, such as monthly.
4. After examining the folder contents, complete the checklist, indicating the extent to which the student demonstrates a specific behavior. For example, is he able to properly sequence story events—always, sometimes, infrequently.

Student Involvement

Students assist by maintaining the folder.

Reporting Techniques

1. Use the checklist as the basis for a letter grade.
   a. Give each rating a number value.
   b. Compute the sum and determine the percentage.
   c. Convert the percentage to a letter grade.
2. Use the checklist to prepare a narrative report.

	Beginning	Developing	Independent	Comments
Before reading				

Makes predictions
    Uses prior knowledge
    Generates questions				

During reading				

Uses picture clues
    Willing to reread
    Self-corrects miscues
    Uses context
    Uses graphophonemic
      cues
    Makes inferences				

After reading				

Makes connections
    Retells adequately
    Summarizes main idea
    Recalls details
    Understands story
      elements
    Understands text
      structure
    Applies information				

For Example

A third grader's mid-year checklist is provided in Figure 10.2. The ratings are based on the contents of his work folder. Note how the teacher has computed his letter grade in reading.

The Literacy Folder System

Purpose

1. To collect samples of students' reading and writing behaviors, including attitudes, print and meaning processing, spelling development, and writing.
2. To monitor students' reading performance by using the contents of the folders as indicators of reading development.

Materials

Individual student folders

Audiotapes

Attitude surveys, for example, The Garfield Elementary Attitude Survey (McKenna & Kear, 1990)

Self-assessment surveys and interest inventories

A hanging file for storing the folders (optional)

FIGURE 10.2
Grade 2 reading checklist

	4 Superior	3 Very Good	2 Adequate	1 Needs Improvement
Attitude				
Enjoys literature		✓		
Chooses to read		✓		
Self-selects appropriately		✓		
Word Recognition				
Uses picture clues	✓			
Uses graphophonemic cues			✓	
Uses syntactic cues		✓		
Uses semantic cues	✓			
Orchestrates cuing systems			✓	
Self-corrects miscues			✓	
Reads fluently			✓	
Comprehension				
Makes predictions		✓		
Confirms predictions			✓	
Understands main idea		✓		
Makes inferences			✓	
Recalls story sequence		✓		
Recalls important details		✓		
Provides summary			✓	
Makes connections		✓		
Score: 49	8	27	14	

Total possible: 72

Percent of total: 68%

Grade: Above Average

General Procedures

1. Provide students with hanging file folders and audiotapes or have students supply their own.
2. Select an array of items to include in the folders at predetermined times of the year, for example:
   - oral reading samples
   - written retelling samples
   - perceptions of reading interview responses
   - writing samples, such as What I Do After School
   - selected daily work papers, such as cloze activities
   - an oral retelling sample
   - an attitude survey
   - spelling samples
   - an interest inventory
   - self-assessment surveys
3. Provide time to collect data on each student at different times throughout the year, for example, beginning, middle, end.
4. Create a chart to record students' performance in the following areas: attitude and interests, perceptions of reading process, print processing, meaning processing, spelling stage, and writing.
5. Decide on a means of rating the students' performance, for example, above average, average, below average.
6. Schedule conferences with the students periodically, using the folder as a springboard for discussion.

Student Involvement

1. Students assist in maintaining the folder.
2. Students provide input in the form of self-assessment devices.
3. Students are made aware of their own performance through periodic conferences.

Reporting Techniques

1. Use the folder as a basis for providing feedback to students.
2. Use it as an information source during parent conferences.
3. Use it as a basis for assigning a letter grade in reading.
   - Give each rating a number value.
   - Assign a number to each item.
   - Compute the student's score in each category.
   - Convert the score to a percentage.
   - Convert the percentage to a letter grade.
   - Average the grades to determine an overall letter grade.
4. Use it as a basis for writing a narrative report.

For Example

Based on the contents of her literacy folder, a fifth grader's beginning-of-the-year performance in six areas is indicated in Figure 10.3. Notice how initially the teacher used a continuum in each area to rate the child's performance. Later, the teacher converted these ratings to numbers to compute a percent for each area. Averaging these, she then determined a grade for this fifth grader.

FIGURE 10.3
Continua for evaluating
literacy folders

	1	2	3	4
	Little	Some	Adequate	Superior

Attitudes and Interests

Demonstrates positive
attitude |---X----|

Demonstrates range of
interests |-------------------------------------X----------------------|

Self-selects books |-------------------------------------X----------------------|

Shares own reading |--X-----------|

Perceptions of Reading

Expresses meaning-based
beliefs |---X------|

Views reading as
information source |---X------|

Views self as active in
reading process |---X------|

Expresses use of multiple
cuing systems |--------------------------------X--------------------------|

Print Processing

Demonstrates use of
multiple cues |-----------------------------------X-----------------|

Demonstrates fluency in
oral reading |---X-----|

Demonstrates accuracy in
oral reading |-----------------------------------X-----------------|

Self-corrects |-----------------------------------X-----------------|

Meaning Processing

Provides gist of passage
read |---X----|

Comprehends at multiple
levels |-------------------------------------X--------------|

Provides substantive
retellings |-------------------------------------X--------------|

Links reading to content
learning |-------------------------------------X--------------|

Writing and Spelling Development

Demonstrates sense of
audience |-------------------------------------X--------------|

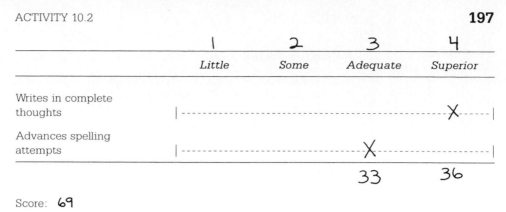

	1 Little	2 Some	3 Adequate	4 Superior
Writes in complete thoughts				X
Advances spelling attempts			X	

33   36

Score: 69

Total possible: 76

Percent of total: 91%

Grade: A

The Literacy Portfolio System

Purposes

1. To provide for the systematic and ongoing collection of reading and writing work, representing multiple indicators of achievement.
2. To select items from the collection that showcase an individual's literacy achievements.
3. To fully involve students in the assessment and evaluation process.

Materials

Individual student folders or hanging files

General Procedures

1. Introduce portfolios as the students' property.
2. Establish a procedure for collecting students' work.
3. With students, brainstorm and list possible items, then set limits as to the number of items that can be included in a showcase portfolio.
4. Provide time for students to select items for their portfolios and to explain why the items were chosen.
5. Periodically review each student's portfolio, commenting about strengths and needs that you notice.
6. Conduct portfolio conferences to examine progress and to instruct and set new goals.
7. With students, generate criteria for evaluating portfolio contents.
8. Involve parents in portfolio reviews by having them examine and comment on portfolio items.

Student Involvement

1. Students assume responsibility for their own work.
2. They select items for their portfolios.
3. They assist in evaluating the items in their portfolios.
4. They participate in discussions about their work.
5. They set goals for themselves.

Reporting Techniques

1. Use the portfolios to involve students in generating criteria for evaluating their own reading and writing performance.
2. Use portfolios for the informal assessment of student progress in literacy.
3. Use portfolios for student self-assessment of literacy behavior.
4. Use portfolios as a parent information resource about literacy growth.

For Example

An example of a portfolio analysis is provided in Figure 10.4. Notice the assessment guide to the left of the analysis as well as the narrative form used to provide feedback. How do you think this information might be converted into a letter grade?

Compare/Contrast Graphic Organizer

Directions: Using the provided frame, jot down the main characteristics of the three systems described on the previous pages.

Features	*Work folder and checklist system*	*Literacy folder system*	*Literacy portfolio system*
Purposes			
Procedures			
Student Involvement			
Reporting			

What to Do Next: Summarize the similarities and differences between these three systems. Use the cloze procedure as a writing guide, but realize that you do not have to conform to it exactly as is. Feel free to remove some parts and add others. In the end, you should have written a concise summary that highlights similar and contrasting features of the three systems.

_____ , _____ , and

_____ are similar in several ways. All _____

_____ and _____ have similar _____

_____ . Finally, all are _____ .

FIGURE 10.4
Sample portfolio analysis

Portfolio Analysis

Name: Molly

Date: Fall

Overall

Well-organized – 3 pieces of writing: 2 expository, 1 personal narrative.
Table of contents for reading and writing sides.
Variety of books read – 7 total.
Self-evaluation – brief but specific to each piece.
Sets goals.
Highly invested in developing her portfolio.

Reading Strengths/Needs

Responses – mostly retelling. Includes primary characters and major events. Good supporting details. Reading a lot!
Good personal reflection. Interest high.
Could take more personal stance in journal.

Writing Strengths/Needs

3 pieces – all include personal evaluation. * wants help with paragraphing. Writing has beginning, middle, end. Strong voice.
Sentence-level errors.
Informational piece - includes use of variety of sources. Good details.

Types of Reading/Writing
- •Projects
- •Genres
- •Selection

Process
- •Goal Setting
- •Problem Solving
- •Engagement
- •Use of Resources
- •Troubleshooting

Self-evaluation
- •Analysis
- •Ongoing Goals

Improvement, Effort, Motivation
Other:

Types of Reading
Process
- •Planning
- •Comprehension Strategies
- •Engagement
- •Decoding and Troubleshooting
- •Versatility

Reading-writing relationship
Reflection and reconsideration
Self-evaluation
- •Analysis
- •Ongoing Goals
- •Motivation

Other:

Types of Writing
Process
- •Planning
- •Problem Solving and Troubleshooting
- •Revision
- •Use of Resources (peers, books)

Reflection and reconsideration
Self-evaluation
- •Analysis
- •Ongoing Goals
- •Motivation

Other:

Note: From *Portfolio Assessment in the Reading/Writing Classroom* (p. 129) by R. Tierney, M. Carter, and L. Desai, 1991, Norwood, MA: Christopher Gordon. Reprinted by permission.

On the other hand, these systems are different in several ways. First of all,

_____ , while _____ .

Second, _____ but _____

In addition, while _____ , _____ .

Finally, _____ .

What to Do Last: Choose one of the three systems and provide a rationale for your choice. You may find the following writing guide useful for this purpose.

I chose _____ because (1) it _____ (2) it _____ and

(3) it _____ .

FOLLOW-UP DISCUSSION

There are at least three ways to organize and maintain diagnostic information: a work folder/checklist system, a literacy folder system, and a literacy portfolio approach.

Through this activity, you became acquainted with three ways to organize and maintain diagnostic information, which, in the end, contributes to the overall assessment and evaluation teachers must do. We need to reiterate, though, that this is merely an introduction. As an educator, you need to be a full participant in the discussions that surround assessment, so we encourage you to read more about literacy assessment and diagnostic information organization. To get you started, we have provided a "must read" list in the Further Reading section at the end of this chapter. Take some time to locate these selections and to read them. If assessment of student achievement in literacy is to reflect the teaching you will soon do, then you must have a voice in its creation. To have such a voice, however, implies a knowledge base from which educationally useful and valid measures of student literacy learning may be derived. Reading some of the selections listed is your invitation to join the discussion and to become involved in improving assessment practices.

Summary

Following a brief discussion of general guidelines and procedures for organizing and managing diagnostic information, three information management systems were described: the work folder/checklist system, the literacy folder, and the literacy portfolio. You were asked to select one of these and to provide a rationale for your choice.

As a beginning teacher, you will need to consider how you will gather, maintain, and use diagnostic information for assessment and evaluation purposes. The three systems described in this chapter may help you in meeting this responsibility, pointing the way toward the sound and humane assessment of children's reading growth.

In addition, the activities in this chapter brought you face-to-face with one of the realities of diagnosis and assessment, namely, becoming familiar with the essential skills of information management. As you continue teaching, you will also continue to refine these skills in your effort to assist readers in their desire and need to read on their own.

Further Reading

Au, K., Scheu, J., Kawakami, A., & Herman, P. (1990). Assessment and accountability in a whole literacy curriculum. *The Reading Teacher, 43,* (8), 574–581. Discusses assessment procedures that are compatible with a whole literacy curriculum as well as accountable to external demands.

Goodman, K., Goodman, Y., & Hood, W. (1989). *The whole language evaluation book.* Portsmouth, NH: Heinemann. Describes the theory and general principles of whole language-based assessment, with supporting "how-to" articles.

Holdaway, D. (1980). *Independence in reading.* Portsmouth, NH: Heinemann. Provides a comprehensive listing of literacy targets for the elementary school years.

Johnston, P. (1992). *Constructive evaluation of literacy activity.* New York: Longman. Presents a constructive view of evaluation as an interpretive and socially interactive activity, involving the noticing of details, themes, and patterns in reading behavior.

Paris, S. (1991). Portfolio assessment for young readers. *The Reading Teacher, 44,* (9), 680–682. Describes a program of portfolio assessment designed for primary-level readers, providing specific assessment tasks.

Tierney, R., Carter, M., Desai, L. (1991). *Portfolio assessment in the reading/writing classroom.* Norwood, MA: Christopher Gordon. Discusses the concept of portfolios as an approach to assessment and provides ample examples of portfolio assessment from actual classrooms.

Valencia, S. (1990). A portfolio approach to classroom reading assessment: The whys, whats and hows. *The Reading Teacher, 43,* (4), 338–340. Overviews the portfolio approach to assessment, providing fundamentals related to it.

Weaver, C. (1988). *Reading process and practice* (Chapters 10–11, pp. 321–409). Portsmouth, NH: Heinemann. Describes basic assessment procedures (e.g., miscue analysis) as well as major reading intervention programs (e.g., reading recovery).

Glossary

Analysis   A mental activity that involves taking things apart, examining each part, then considering how the parts relate to one another and to the whole.

Authenticity   Instructional and assessment activities that replicate real-life situations.

Balance   As a lesson design factor, provides stability and equilibrium in learning.

Basal   A reading program, based on anthologies of graded text, to teach reading skills.

Bender Visual-Motor Gestalt Test for Children   An individually administered test that measures visual-motor integration.

Central method of word attack   A technique of word solving where the reader focuses on content and beginning letters, checking by sense and letter detail.

Choral reading   An instructional technique that uses unison or choral reading of poems and plays in the classroom.

Cloze activity   An instructional technique in which target words are deleted from a selection, then students are encouraged to think about what would make sense in the sentence and in the entire story.

Coherence   Reading activities that are connected, congruent, and consistent with the goals of the lesson and the strengths and needs of the reader.

Concepts about print   The emerging knowledge about how print works, for example, reading left to right, where the words are on the page, and where a word begins and ends.

Confirm   Checking guesses to see if they fit with the text and with what students know.

Constructive process   A process of making predictions and confirming them while integrating the printed information with what we already know.

Content area DR-TA   An assessment tool that indicates how a reader predicts, confirms, and integrates expository (informational) text.

Content area reading-informal (CARI)   A reading assessment that measures reading performance in the content area.

Continuous diagnostic assessment   A time in the lesson where assessment tools and procedures are used to examine reading behaviors.

Convention   Conforming to the standard forms of English.

Critical thinking   Taking ideas apart, selecting important aspects, and then reorganizing the ideas to affect action or make a point.

Directed listening-thinking activity (DL-TA)   An instructional and informal assessment tool to observe and develop prediction, confirmation, and integration strategies while listening to stories.

Directed reading activity (DRA)   An instructional technique in which the teacher develops and activates background knowledge, introduces unfamiliar vocabulary words, and sets the purpose for reading. The teacher also directs the discussion with literal and inferential comprehension questions.

Directed reading-thinking activity (DR-TA)   An instructional and informal assessment procedure to observe and develop prediction, confirmation, and summarization strategies while reading stories.

Dynamic   Ongoing and continually changing.

Early phonemic stage   A stage of spelling development in which students represent whole words by one or more letters that indicate some of the sounds in the words; invented spelling is limited.

Elementary Reading Attitude Survey   A quick indicator of student attitudes toward recreational and academic reading.

Expository text   Informational text used in the content area.

Familiar text time   A time in the lesson in which readers use passages and stories they have already read and know well.

Fluency   Reading in phrases with a good sense of rhythm; usually there are only a few repetitions, and these are made to correct phrasing errors rather than word recognition errors.

Fluency rating scale   A 4-point rating scale for evaluating children's reading fluency.

Formal assessment tools   Testing tools that sample reading performance on a prescribed task at one point in time, and then describe this performance based on its relationship to a normative or representative group of readers.

Frustration level   A level of text that is so demanding and difficult that a reader is unable to construct meaning.

Gates-MacGinitie Reading Test   A standardized survey reading test that measures vocabulary and comprehension.

Graphic organizer   A sort of "picture" of how ideas and main concepts are related in a content-area chapter.

Graphophonemic   A cue system based on how sounds, or phonemes, and symbols, or graphemes, work in the English language; it is our phonic knowledge.

Guided imagery   A technique which uses sensory images to activate background knowledge about situations or concepts in the text.

Heathington Attitude Surveys   An assessment tool that measures attitude toward different reading situations, such as free reading.

Independent level   A level of text where the reader processes text rapidly and easily. This is so familiar that it doesn't need instruction.

Informal assessment tools   Structured tests that use observations to analyze reading behaviors.

Informal reading inventory   An informal assessment that measures print and meaning processing on a series of graded passages; establishes independent, instructional, and frustration levels of reading.

Instructional level   A level of text where the reader needs assistance from the teacher or a more capable peer. This text is somewhat challenging.

Integrate   Combining new information and strategies with what is already known.

Interest inventory   An informal assessment to reveal specific reading interests.

Interpretation   To infer and summarize reader strengths and needs based on an understanding of literacy development.

Invented spelling   Spellings of words that represent the sounds of the words rather than the conventional form.

Inventive   Rediscovering the functions and rules of written language.

Jigsaw   A method for using cooperative learning groups in which each group becomes an expert on a specific case or unit. After studying, new groups are formed that contain at least one expert from each previous group.

Journal writing   A flexible instructional technique in which students write daily about what they are reading or simply write about their ideas and feelings.

Language-experience approach   An instructional technique, used primarily with beginning readers, in which the student dictates a story to the teacher. This story then becomes the instructional passage for the student. The stories can be collected and put into an anthology.

Learning log   A log or journal in which the student writes about what is read and learned in specific content areas.

Letter-naming stage   Students' writing in this stage includes sounds represented by the letter name, with more than half the sounds represented. This is often referred to as invented spelling.

Literature-based reading program   A reading program that uses quality children's books instead of basal readers, and children interact and discuss these books in groups or in individual conferences with the teacher.

Meaning processing   The reader's effort to process the deeper meaning of the text; how readers comprehend the author's message.

Message writing   An instructional technique in which the student thinks of a message to write and slowly says the words, predicting the letters in each word. The teacher assists with an unknown or incorrect word by drawing boxes to represent each letter of the word, and then lets the student fill in the boxes he/she knows.

Metacomprehension Index   A questionnaire to measure the reader's awareness of comprehension strategies.

Milestones   General patterns and significant points in children's literacy development.

Miscue   When the reader deviates from what is actually printed.

Names Test   A test of decoding ability.

New text time   A time in the lesson in which a new story or passage is presented, providing a challenge to the reader.

Norms   Based on the normal curve, which means that 68% of the population at a certain age will fall within the average range. This provides a representative comparison.

Observation   Examining actual literacy behaviors.

Peabody Picture Vocabulary Test   An individually administered test that measures the student's receptive vocabulary, or those words he or she can recognize in a pictorial rendition.

Perceptions about reading   The personal definition that each person has about how the reading process works, for example, reading for meaning, calling the words, or constructing responses.

Personalized reading and writing   Reading and writing for individual purposes.

Portfolio   A folder or packet that contains multiple samples of reading and writing experiences, used to depict a student's reading performance and growth over time.

Pragmatic system   A cue system based on how language is used in different situations; it is our situational knowledge.

Predict and confirm   An instructional technique in which the teacher deletes words from a short selection written on the board, then orally presents this selection, saying "Gugglefunk" for each missing word. Students predict what words would make sense in place of the nonsense word.

Predictable books   Books that contain repetitious patterns and supportive pictures so that students can easily predict the words in the text.

Prediction   Making guesses about what the text will say.

Prephonemic stage   Students' writing in this stage exhibits a left-to-right concept, letter forms that represent a message, and known letters written accurately. There is little resemblance between letters and sounds.

Print orientation assessment   An informal measure of young children's concept about how print works.

Print processing   The reader's attempt to process the printed text by using the syntactic, graphophonemic, semantic, and pragmatic cue systems. Encompasses the traditional areas of sight-word recognition, word analysis, decoding, using context clues, and fluency.

Procedures   Guides that teachers use to facilitate the analysis and summarization of information collected about an individual's reading behaviors.

Process of diagnosis   The mental activity associated with making decisions about individuals' reading behaviors.

Process-oriented   Activities and assessments that focus on the process of active reading, or how readers are constructing meaning.

Product-oriented   Activities and assessments that show *what* the reader accomplished— what he or she knows (skills, strategies, etc.), but not *how* he or she knows it.

Psychoeducational assessments   Contrived reading and learning tasks that measure both cognitive abilities and academic achievement. These assessments are administered individually in a one-to-one setting and are reported in terms of how a student performed in relationship to a representative sample.

Rationales   Reasons for choosing activities based on observations, analyses, and interpretations.

Reader-based information   Information that the reader already knows.

Reading interview   An informal procedure in which the reader is asked questions about the reading process as well as perceptions and beliefs about reading.

Reflection   A mental activity that involves reconsidering actions in order to clarify and expand knowledge about teaching and to improve student learning.

Reliability   Test results that can be duplicated.

ReQuest technique   An instructional technique where the teacher and the students take turns asking and answering questions as they read a story.

Retelling   An instructional and assessment procedure in which readers are asked to recount what they read as if they were telling it to a friend.

Retrospective repeated readings   An instructional technique in which the student re-reads text. After the first reading, the teacher and student discuss the miscues and how to self-correct these, emphasizing the text cues and the reader's own knowledge related to the specific miscue.

Rubric   A scale developed with criteria of performance that measures the specific task being measured.

Running record   An informal tool in which the teacher can observe the cueing system (semantic, syntactic, graphophonemic) the reader uses for print processing.

Scaffolds   Actions taken by the teacher or peer to encourage active reading. These actions include such activities as leading questions, modeling, cooperative tasks, and prompts.

Schemata   Background knowledge that provides connections which frame and integrate text information.

Scoreable miscue   An oral reading error that significantly disrupts the author's intended meaning; may be used to compute an error rate.

Self-assessment   A time when readers review their own reading performance and begin to evaluate what they know and can do.

Self-directed questioning   An instructional technique in which the teacher models his/her internal dialogue, using questions like: What must I do? What did the text say? and What do I know about that? After the modeling, students are asked to think aloud, using the self-directed questions.

Semantic mapping   An instructional technique in which the teacher or students place the target word in the center of a page, then arrange related words and concepts around the word to show relationships among what they already know and the new word or concept.

Semantic system   A cue system that uses the meaning of the text.

Shared reading   An instructional technique in which the teacher and students read predictable books together, with the teacher taking the lead and the students filling in the familiar words in the predictable pattern of the text.

Sight-word list   An informal assessment tool that contains a graded list of words which the student reads at sight; this determines how automatically the student recognizes words.

Skill and strategy instruction   A time during a session in which the teacher uses a minilesson to show students how to use needed skills and strategies.

Speech-to-print match   An informal assessment tool used to observe how the student can match oral language to printed text.

Spelling features   An informal assessment of a student's stage of spelling development.

Standardized assessments   Testing tools that sample reading performance on a prescribed task at one point in time, and then describe this performance based on its relationship to a normative or representative group of readers.

Story frame   A large cloze activity in which students are asked to generate the setting, the main character, the problem, the events, and the resolution.

Story structure   How stories are formed, that is, the grammar of the story.

Syntactic system   A cue system based on how language is put together, or the structure of sentences.

Text-based information   Information that is found directly in the text.

Theorizing   The mental activity involved in creating a solution to a problem.

Three-level guide   An instructional technique in which the teacher constructs a study guide containing questions at three levels (literal, interpretive, and applied) about the content of a chapter in an expository text.

Tools   Real objects used to get jobs done; in the role of teaching, assessment tasks are the tools used.

Transitional stage   A stage of spelling development in which conventional rules are used appropriately, but not correctly; for example, a student might write "littel" for "little".

Translation   To transfer our interpretations into another form, such as actual instruction or reports to parents, colleagues, and children.

Validity   Does the text measure what it says it measures.

Warm ups   Brief experiences with print that help readers ease into the challenge of reading.

***Wechsler Intelligence Scale for Children-Revised* (WISC-R)**   A norm-referenced test of general intellectual functioning that samples performance on verbal (tapping language use) and performance (tapping visual understanding) tasks and yields a full-scale score of intellectual functioning.

Whole language   An approach to reading instruction that focuses on watching the child as he/she reads and writes about self-selected children's literature.

Wide Range Achievement Test - Revised   A quick assessment of achievement level in which the reading subtest consists of letter recognition, letter naming, and isolated reading of words on a page. No information is gathered regarding students' oral reading accuracy or comprehension.

Woodcock-Johnson Psycho-Educational Battery—Part Two   An individually administered, norm-referenced test designed to diagnose students' mastery of various academic subjects. The Reading Cluster consists of three subtests, letter-word identification, word attack, and passage comprehension.

Word caller   A student who simply says the words in the text without thinking of the meaning.

Word sort   An activity in which students sort word cards according to specific attributes. An open word sort is where the students group the words and define the attribute. A closed word sort is where the teacher gives the students the cards and has them sort by a specific attribute.

Writing samples   Examples of an individual's writing over time.

Writing workshop   An instructional approach in which students write every day, keeping their rough drafts in folders. From these drafts, they choose drafts to revise and edit.

References

Baskwill, J. (1989). *The whole language source book.* New York: Scholastic.

Bender, L. (1962). *Bender visual-motor gestalt test for children.* New York: The Psychological Corporation.

Bissex, G. (1980). *Gyns at work: A child learns to read and write.* Cambridge, MA: Harvard University Press.

Blume, J. (1971). *Freckle juice.* New York: Four Winds.

Brophy, J. (1984). The teacher as thinker: Implementing instruction. In G. Duffy, L. Roehler, & J. Mason (Eds.), *Comprehension instruction: Perspectives and suggestions* (pp. 71–92). New York: Longman.

Brown, A. (1985). Metacognition: The development of selective attention strategies for learning from texts. In H. Singer & R. Ruddell (Eds.), *Theoretical models and processes of reading* (3rd ed.) (pp. 501–526). Newark, DE: International Reading Association.

Burgess, G. (1961). *The purple cow.* New York: Dover.

California Achievement Test. (1992). Monterey, CA: McGraw-Hill.

Cambourne, B. (1990, November). *An ecological perspective of literacy acquisition.* Paper presented at the 40th annual meeting of the National Reading Conference, Miami, FL.

Cave, H. (1989). Two were left. In B. Goodman (Ed.), *Sudden twists: 18 tales that take a surprising turn.* Providence, RI: Jamestown.

Cazden, C. (1981). *Language in early childhood education.* Washington, DC: National Association for the Education of Young Children (NAEYC).

Clay, M. (1967). The reading behavior of five year old children: A research report. *New Zealand Journal of Educational Studies, 2* (1), 11–31.

Clay, M. (1985). *The early detection of reading difficulties: A diagnostic survey with recovery procedures* (2nd ed.). Portsmouth, NH: Heinemann.

Cochrane, O., Cochrane, D., Scalena, S., & Buchanen, E. (1984). *Reading, writing and caring.* New York: Richard Owens.

Cunningham, P. (1990). The names test: A quick assessment of decoding ability. *The Reading Teacher, 44* (2), 124–129.

Dahl, R. (1970). *Fantastic Mr. Fox.* New York: Alfred Knopf.

Downing, J. (1979). *Reading and reasoning.* New York: Springer-Verlag.

Dunn, L. M. (1981). *Peabody picture vocabulary test - revised.* Circle Pines, MN: American Guidance Service.

Eastman, P. D. (1960). *Are you my mother?* New York: Random House.

Eisner, E. (1990). Who decides what schools teach? *Phi Delta Kappan, 71* (2), 523–526.

Eisner, E., & Valance, E. (Eds.). (1974). *Conflicting conceptions of curriculum.* Berkeley: McCutchan.

Eliot, T. S. (1941). *The dry salvages.* New York: Faber and Faber.

Ferreiro, E., & Teberosky, A. (1982). *Literacy before schooling.* Portsmouth, NH: Heinemann.

Galdone, P. (1975). *The little red hen.* New York: Scholastic.

Gates, A. I., & MacGinitie, W. H. (1989). *Gates-MacGinitie Reading Tests* (3rd ed.). Chicago, IL: Riverside.

Gillet, J., & Temple, C. (1990). *Understanding reading problems* (3rd ed.). Glenview, IL: Scott-Foresman.

Gilman, P. (1985). *Jillian Jiggs.* New York: Scholastic.

Glazer, S., & Searfoss, L. (1988). *Reading diagnosis and instruction: A C.A.L.M. approach.* Englewood Cliffs, NJ: Prentice-Hall.

Goodman, K., Bird, L., & Goodman, Y. (1991). *The whole language catalog.* Santa Rosa, CA: American School Publishers.

Goodman, Y., & Burke, C. (1980, 1987). *Reading strategies: Focus on comprehension.* New York: Richard C. Owen.

Harlin, R., Lipa, S., & Lonberger, R. (1991). *The whole language journey.* Markham, Ontario: Pippin.

Harris, A., & Sipay, E. (1980). *How to increase reading ability* (7th ed.). New York: Longman.

Heathington, B. (1975). *The development of scales to measure attitudes toward reading.* Unpublished doctoral dissertation, University of Tennessee, Knoxville.

Hoberman, M. A. (1986). *A house is a house for me.* New York: Scholastic.

Holdaway, D. (1979). *The foundations of literacy.* Portsmouth, NH: Heinemann.

Jastak, J. F., & Jastak, S. R. (1984). *Wide range achievement test-revised.* Wilmington, DE: Guidance Associates.

Johnston, P. H. (1984). Assessment in reading. In P. D. Pearson (Ed.), *Handbook of reading research* (pp. 147–182). New York: Longman.

Lidtke, M. (1991). Don't pick that scab. *Highlights for Children, 46,* p. 18.

Lobel, A. (1972). *Frog and toad together.* New York: Harper.

Manzo, T. (1969). The ReQuest procedure. *Journal of Reading, 2,* 123–126.

McGovern, A. (1967). *Too much noise.* New York: Scholastic.

McGuire, L. (1981). *This farm is a mess.* New York: Parents Magazine.

McKenna, M., & Kear, D. (1990). Measuring attitude toward reading: A new tool for teachers. *The Reading Teacher, 43* (9), 626–639.

Morrow, L. (1988). Retelling stories as a diagnostic tool. In S. Glazer, L. Searfoss, & L. Gentile (Eds.), *Re-examining reading diagnosis: New trends and procedures.* Newark, DE: International Reading Association.

Munsch, R. (1990). *Love you forever.* Willowdale, Ontario: Firefly Books.

Ness, E. (1966). *Sam, Bangs and Moonshine.* New York: Holt, Rinehart & Winston.

Newman, Cardinal John (1848, June 27). Letter to Mrs. William Froude. In *The Oxford dictionary of quotations* (3rd ed.). New York: Oxford University Press.

Paulsen, G. (1991). *The boy who owned the school.* New York: Dell.

Pearson, P. D., & Johnson, D. (1978). *Teaching reading comprehension.* New York: Holt, Rinehart & Winston.

Piaget, J. (1962). *The psychology of the child.* New York: Basic Books.

Piaget, J. (1972). *To understand is to invent.* New York; Grossman.

Porter, F. (1981). In D. Koberg and J. Bagnall, *The all new universal traveler.* Los Altos, CA: William Kaufman.

Potter, B. (n.d.). *The tale of Peter Rabbit.* London: Warne.

Quackenbush, R. (1980). *Henry's awful mistake.* New York: Parents Magazine.

Resnick, L. (1990). Literacy in school and out. *Daedelus, 119* (2), 169–185.

Rogoff, B. (1989). *Apprenticeship in thinking.* New York: Oxford University Press.

Schickedanz, J. (1986). *More than the ABC's: The early stages of reading and writing.* Washington, DC: National Association for the Education of Young Children.

Schmitt, M. (1990). A questionnaire to measure children's awareness of strategic reading processes. *The Reading Teacher, 43* (7), 454–463.

Schon, D. (1987). *Educating the reflective practitioner.* San Francisco: Jossey-Bass.

Schwartz, A. (1984). *More scary stories to tell in the dark.* New York: HarperCollins.

Schwartz, A. (1991). *Scary Stories 3: More tales to chill your bones.* New York: HarperCollins.

Silverstein, S. (1974). *Where the sidewalk ends.* New York: Harper-Row.

Smith, F. (1978). *Understanding reading* (2nd ed.). New York: Holt, Rinehart & Winston.

Smith, H., & Dechant, E. (1961). *Psychology in teaching reading.* Englewood Cliffs, NJ: Prentice-Hall.

Sobol, D. (1973). *Encyclopedia Brown takes a case.* Nashville, TN: Thomas Nelson.

Sulzby, E. (1985). Children's emergent reading of favorite storybooks: A developmental study. *Reading Research Quarterly, 20,* 458–481.

Thompson, D. B. (1966). This is Halloween. In B. Martin (Ed.), *Sounds of laughter.* New York: Holt, Rinehart & Winston.

Vacca, R., & Vacca, J. (1989). *Content area reading* (chapter 2). Glenview, IL: Scott, Foresman.

Van Allen, R. (1985). *I love ladybugs.* Austin, TX: DLM Teaching Resources.

Vygotsky, L. (1962). *Thought and language* (E. Hanfmann & G. Vakar, Trans.) Cambridge, MA: MIT Press.

Vygotsky, L. S. (1978). *Mind in society.* Cambridge, MA: Harvard University Press.

Walker, B. (1992a). *Diagnostic teaching of reading: Techniques for instruction and assessment.* New York: Merrill/Macmillan.

Walker, B. (1992b). *Supporting struggling readers.* Markham, Ontario, Pippin.

Walker, B. J. (1990). A model for diagnostic narrative in teacher education. In N. Padak, T. Rasinski, & J. Logan (Eds.), *Challenges in reading* (pp. 1–10). Pittsburg, KS: College Reading Association.

Walker, B. J. (1991). *A descriptive study of the reflective statements of preservice teachers.* In N. Padak, T. Rasinski, & J. Logan (Eds.), *Reading is knowledge* (pp. 98–103). Pittsburg, KS: College Reading Association.

Weaver, C. (1988). *Reading process and practice: From socio-psycholinguistics to whole language* (pp. 206–207). Portsmouth, NH: Heinemann.

Weschsler, D. (1974). *Weschler intelligence scale for children-revised.* New York: Psychological Corporation.

Wells, R. (1973). *Noisy Nora.* New York: Scholastic.

Whole earth catalog. (1971). Bladensburg, MD: Craftsman Press.

Woodcock, R. W., & Johnson, M. B. (1977). *Woodcock-Johnson psychoeducational battery-revised.* Boston: Teaching Resources.

Yinger, R. J. (1979). Routines in teacher planning. *Theory into Practice, 18,* 163–169.

Zutell, J. (1988, May). *Developing a procedure for assessing oral reading fluency: Establishing validity and reliability.* Paper presented at the 33rd annual meeting of the International Reading Conference, Toronto, Canada.

Index

The Authors

Kathy Roskos is an associate professor and chair of the Department of Education at John Carroll University, where she also teaches undergraduate and graduate courses in language arts and reading. She received her Ph.D. from Kent State University specializing in early literacy development and reading instruction. Her research interests include young children's literacy development, relationships between literacy and play, and reading pedagogy. Prior to college teaching, Dr. Roskos was a reading teacher in the elementary schools and a program administrator of Chapter One, Special Education Services, and Adult Basic Education. She is currently an associate editor of *The Reading Teacher* and participates in various professional organizations, including the International Reading Association, the Association for the Study of Play, the American Educational Research Association, and the National Reading Conference.

Barbara J. Walker is professor and chair of the Department of Special Education and Reading at Eastern Montana College, where she also coordinates the Reading Clinic. Dr. Walker was a distinguished finalist for the International Reading Association's 1991 Albert J. Harris Award, and was the 1987 recipient of the Eastern Montana College Faculty Achievement Award for scholarship and creativity. She received her Ed.D. from Oklahoma State University in Curriculum and Instruction specializing in reading disabilities. Her publications include *Diagnostic Teaching of Reading: Techniques for Instruction and Assessment*, Second Edition and *Supporting Struggling Readers*. Her research on individual assessment, learning styles, imagery instruction and teacher education has been published in various reading journals and yearbooks. Before entering college teaching, Dr. Walker was a reading specialist in the elementary schools of Stillwater, Oklahoma; organized and taught in the college reading program at Vernon Regional Junior College in Vernon, Texas; and coordinated the educational program at the Hogar Paul Harris in Cochabamba, Bolivia.

Dr. Walker is a frequent presenter at state, regional, and national reading conferences, where she speaks on individual differences in the acquisition of literacy. She is active in various professional organizations, including the Montana State Reading Council, the International Reading Association, the College Reading Association, where she is on the Board of Directors, and the National Reading Conference.

ISBN 0-02-423730-2

9 780024 237309

90000>